Into The Great Below

A Devotional To Inanna And Ereshkigal

Galina Krasskova

Into The Great Below

A Devotional
For Inanna And Ereshkigal

With Selected Prayers To Other Sumerian Deities

Galina Krasskova

Galina Krasskova (signature)

Asphodel Press

Hubbardston, Massachusetts

Asphodel Press
12 Simond Hill Road
Hubbardston, MA 01452

Into The Great Below: A Devotional For Inanna And Ereshkigal
© 2010 by Galina Krasskova
ISBN 978-0-9825798-3-1

Cover Art by Abby Helasdottir
Artwork on p. 23 by Meq
Artwork on pp. 4, 5, 11, 12, 15, 20, 31, 33,
80, 90, and 120 by Abby Helasdottir
Photo on p. 29 by Kipof
All others public domain

Printed in cooperation with
Lulu Enterprises, Inc.
860 Aviation Parkway, Suite 300
Morrisville, NC 27560

To those who once served these goddesses,
To those who will serve now,
And to those who will serve again
I give this book.

Contents

Part III: Rituals To Inanna And Ereshkigal

Foreword

I am a devout Heathen. I'm owned by Odin and have fairly extensive devotions to a plethora of other Norse Gods. As a Heathen, I rarely venture outside of the Norse pantheon. So what am I doing writing a devotional to Sumerian Gods? The answer to that question is rather convoluted, but in the end, what it comes down to is simple: I owe both Inanna and Ereshkigal a great debt.

I did not begin my spiritual life as a Heathen; indeed, few of us in this generation of the community did. I first came into Paganism through the aegis of the Fellowship of Isis. I was very, very lucky in that I found an amazing Iseum with which to work quite soon after my conversion. Within that Iseum, for several years, I was mentored by a priestess of Inanna. This mentoring laid in me a foundation through which I could confidently grow in faith, service, and from which I might have the courage to follow wherever my Gods might lead. That is not an insignificant gift. From this woman I learned ritual work, how to run a group, how to properly lay an altar, and how to honor the Gods. From her, I learned to find joy in worship. From her example and teaching, I learned that truly as Rumi once wrote, "there are hundreds of ways to kneel and kiss the ground." That was Inanna's gift to me; She kindled in me the fire of priesthood. Through Her emissary, this magnificent Goddess was one of my earliest teachers.

It wasn't until I began my own group that I had the opportunity to learn at Ereshkigal's feet. This time there was no intermediary. The barest glimpse that I was granted of Her wisdom, power, and beauty was enough to kindle in me a deep love and respect for this Goddess, though I am not Hers. I use the gifts She taught me every single day in my work as a shaman. Because of Her, I am better able to serve Odin efficiently and well. She taught me before I even realized I was being taught. What did I learn from Her? She was my oh-so-subtle entry into the art and craft of Ordeal. She taught me to create rituals that would challenge the spirit; She taught me how to confront the ego, how to use psychodrama to open initiates to the Gods, how to dance with and work through fear. Most of all, She taught to create, navigate, and work with a state of sacred vulnerability into which the Gods might reach. She taught me to do this, as safely as it can be done, and always with respect. Ereshkigal showed me the necessity of always hammering away at my own ego. She taught me humility. This Goddess set my feet before I ever realized it, on the path of ordeal, and of sacred service. I owe a debt to both of Them and this is my way of beginning its repayment.

This is a very simple devotional. It is not a work of academic scholarship. It is a small collection of prayers and rituals from many different sources, many different devotees united in their desire to honor these two great Goddesses. It's a beginning. I hope over the next few years to see devotionals to the entire Sumerian pantheon. I know Their devotees are out there. It's only a matter of time.

GALINA KRASSKOVA
NEW YORK CITY, NY
MAY 31, 2010

Part I
Devotions
To Inanna
And Ereshkigal

Inanna, the Queen of Heaven
Galina Krasskova

Inanna is the Queen of Heaven in Sumerian cosmology. Her sister Ereshkigal is the Goddess of the underworld. Ereshkigal is, in many respects, an Initiator. As part of Her path to power, Inanna journeyed through seven gates, guarded by terrible sentries to visit Her sister. At each gate, She sacrificed some aspect of Herself, some aspect of Her temporal power. She entered the realm of Her sister naked, "bowed low" as the surviving lore relates. Ereshkigal looked at her and stripped away the last fragments of hubris, pride—Her pride in Her power, Her beauty, Her apparent perfection, and arrogance. She fixed upon Inanna the eye of death and Inanna died. For three days and nights Ereshkigal let Her corpse hang on a meat hook. It wasn't until the intervention of the *galatur* and *kurgurra*, whom the God Enki created specifically to rescue Inanna, that She was recalled to life and freed. This story is called the Descent of Inanna. While surviving stories and hymns also celebrate Inanna's passion and sexuality and Her union with Dumuzi, that is not the focus of the prayers and poems below. Here we honor Her relationship with Her sister, here we call to mind the journey of the Goddess of the Great Above, into the Realm of the Great Below.

Aretalogy of Inanna

Rebecca Buchanan

I am Inanna
The Holy One Who Appears in Heaven
(I am clothed in dawn sky and dusk)
Great Lady of Heaven
(The stars are my treasure)
Priestess of Heaven
(I created the holy rites)
Hierodule of Heaven
(My vulva is sacred)
Morning and Evening Star
(I guide the Sun and mark its path)
First Daughter of the Moon
(Eldest and wisest of the Gods)
Queen of Heaven and Earth
(My sister denied me the third realm of creation)
Loud Thundering Storm
(I am the raging torrent that fertilizes the fields)
Amazement of the Land
(All that swims or crawls or flies bows in awe of me)
Holy Shepherdess
(I protect and increase the flocks)
Righteous Judge
(My punishment is swift and true)
Framer of All Decrees
(My laws are just)
Opener of the Womb
(I bring forth babes in blood and pain)
Light of the World
(My radiance is blinding)
Forgiver of Sins
(I offer purity and absolution)
I am Inanna

Prayer to Inanna I
Rebecca Buchanan

Inanna
Coppersmith of the Heart
Take up your tongs
and your hammer
Beat my organ
Forge it with fire
and pain
Make me a heart for passion
and anger
and love
A woman's heart

Hymn to Inanna I

Rebecca Buchanan

Inanna
Devastatrix
Your wings are the storm
Your eyes the lightning
Your voice the thunder
Forests tremble
lions flee
bulls quake
before your majesty
Tempestuous Goddess
Whose storms bring life.

Hymn To Inanna II
Rebecca Buchanan
(after Enheduanna)

Lady
Who is called

Nin
Ninnin
Ninni
Ninnar
Ninanna
Nana
Innina
Irnina
Innini
Innur
Ennin
Ennina
Inanna

Lady
By your many names
I sing your praise.

Invocation To Inanna

First published in Pagan Book of Hours *by the Order of the Horae ,*
Asphodel Press, 2006. Used with permission.
Adapted from a traditional prayer.

I say, "Hail!" to the Holy One who appears in the heavens!
I say, "Hail!" to the Holy Priestess of Heaven!
I say, "Hail!" to Inanna, Great Lady of Heaven!
Holy Torch! You fill the sky with light!
You brighten the day at dawn!
I say, "Hail!" to Inanna, Great Lady of Heaven!
Awesome Lady of the Annuna Gods!
Crowned with great horns,
You fill the heavens and earth with light!
At evening the radiant star, the great light fills the sky,
The Lady of the Evening comes bravely forth from heaven,
The people in all the lands lift their eyes to Her,
The ox in his yoke lows for her,
The sheep stir up the dust in their fold,
The beasts, the many living creatures of the steppe,
The lush gardens and orchards, the green reeds and trees,
The fish of the Deep and the birds of Heaven,
Inanna makes them hurry to their sleeping places.
I say, "Hail!" to Inanna, First Daughter of the Moon!
Mighty, majestic, and radiant,
You shine brilliantly in the evening,
You brighten the day at dawn,
You stand in the heavens like the sun and the moon,
Your wonders are known both above and below,
To the greatness of the Holy Priestess of Heaven,
To you, Inanna, I sing!

For The Queen Of Heaven
Elizabeth Vongvisith

O Lady
Great Queen
Radiant One
with a sword
and a barley-sheaf

Who rises supremely enthroned
above the curve of the world
girded with stars
crowned in
auroras of midnight

Who descends swiftly
shedding robe and crown
scepter and jewels
to hang motionless
upon Your sister's hooks

Beloved Goddess
of whom poets sing
and priestesses chant praise
Ruler of love and war
Inanna most holy

May Your name never be forgotten
never be erased
from human memory
for You were
among the first
to Whom we turned
our loving
longing faces

To Inanna
Byron Ballard, Priestess

I made an altar-promise once. I told Inanna that if she'd fill my rain barrels in two days, I'd adapt a praise-song for Her. I had run an errand and there was a sprinkle of rain that afternoon, but I shook my head at Her and told her that wouldn't be nearly sufficient. It poured later that day and the next day we had an afternoon of rain and storms all day.

What can I say? I kept my bargain. And because it is summer, I've adapted the opening verses of "Ecstasy" for Inanna.

Rituals as the Serpent Uncoils

All acts of love and pleasure
All acts of love and pleasure
All acts of love and pleasure
These are my rituals!
Though clad in black, I shone like the moon.
At the dark end of yesterday, I shone like the moon.
Bright.
As I glowed, as I shone,
As I danced through the rain
And onto the great porch of the Temple,
I was singing.
I sang a song of the coming night, long-awaited.
He rose to meet me.
He rose from his place in the shadow to meet me.
The boy who was rose to meet me
And we embraced on the porch of the Temple.
The boy put his hand in mine.
We are here again.
Together as before, long time before.
I have the evening free
And you have only to go home to your mother.
My thoughts ranged to the night—

Free me of the serpent, wild bull, free me.
Stay away from field and house
And play with me.
You shine in beauty,
You glow as the moon glows in the hills.
I am only in shadow, waiting, always waiting.
Tonight my waiting has been broken with the delight of you.
We will watch the cooling rain from here
But our passion will not be cooled.
The touch of finger on face,
Of lip on nipple, all will be enjoyed.
You must have a place, a quiet place
Where noise of flesh to flesh may joyfully be made.
In this place I will make for you a beautiful bed,
Soft with herbs from the mountains.
There we may play the lapis flute, the bowl of amber.
There the animal calls and the bird calls,
There may the calls of our wild kindred
Be made by the priestess and the boy.

This is my praise-song through the Great Priestess.
This is my praise-song promised in exchange for rain.

I have closed the gate behind me,
The garden is secured from animals
And the beans and melons are there to pick and enjoy.
I have closed the gate behind me
And I walk with a light step, a joyful dancing girl-step.
His work it is to bring the sacred oil,
To drop it slowly on the ground of honor.
Cypress oil, and dragon's blood.
Wine from grapes is his and flesh of boar.
Dumuzzi!
Whose song is joy and bliss,
Whose home smells of good things and of honey.

The boy who was remembers the way to heaven.
He remembers the words of bliss.
Dumuzi!
Lay your head upon my breast.
Sweet is the growth of the vine, permission given.
The taste of thin broth fills my mouth
As the night cools to morning.

This is my praise-song through the Great Priestess.
This is my praise-song promised in exchange for rain.

Inanna's Ride

Rebecca Buchanan

Laughing
She rides the Bull of Heaven
Her legs round his majestic shoulders
      Gugalanna
Tossing stars with his horns
Tearing the sky with his hooves
the great gash
bleeding divine light
      Laughing

Inanna Speaks
Kira R.

(I am, in part, devoted to Ereshkigal but I think that anyone who works for Ereshkigal, who honors Her will inevitably encounter Inanna and vice versa. I received the following after a ritual in which both Goddesses were invoked. I had been doing a great deal of praying over the situation in the Middle East and had asked Inanna what could be done. When She came to me, it was as a fury, enraged, filled with anguish, loss, and sorrow...and anger. I have never experienced anything before or since. This was my attempt to translate into words what I experienced that night.)

Shrieking.
Hear the Goddess, Goddess shrieking.
The vault of heaven shattering, crashing down
Blood spurting from the wound, where vacant pieces fall.
Smell the Goddess, Goddess dying
A thousand, thousand lifetimes, crushed and lost.
Inanna breathing in every one,
Breath clotted torturing Her throat.
Empty Goddess, ripe decay, rotting fruit,
Bodies like cattle, matchsticks piled high
The roar of the furnace...
Naked throat of the priestess defiled
Cut by a Hebrew blade,
Golden calf bleeding
Temple fallen
Rebuilt by unclean hands.
Hear the Goddess, Goddess wailing
Rage and fury, serpent uncoiling
Daughter after daughter bound
Filthy shards of glass raised high
Plunging down, devouring innocent flesh
Mutilating the bodies of the young,
Females sacrificed, scarified

In the name of a weeping God who turns away his face in shame.
Inanna hangs above the abyss,
Swallowing poison, vomiting blood, Her genitals shred
To the sound of chanting imams. Holy writ, their words bound in Her flesh.
Holy carcass, piss and shit, a skin stretched too tightly
To hold the violation of the knowing.

Inanna embraces the abyss,
Opening Her cunt to its cruel thrust,
Raped by demons' dying lust.
Birthing in blood and shit and pain, in ruthless sanctity,
The knowledge that streams like fire
Through the bowels of the world,
Crafted in blissful white bone, scorched in the sun;
In the gore of a thousand childrens' violated flesh.
No room for virgins.
No room for pain.
No room for regret.
Only a knowing that devours that which would devour.

She takes all into Herself.
She is both defiler and defiled.
She is plague and sickness, AIDS and Ebola,
Festering, running wounds on the body of a child.
She is the spurting cock of a rapist,
The bleeding tears of the victim,
The fury of the land at its abuse.
She is the child whose body is plundered,
The madness of the plunderer,
And with cold certainty She bears witness.
She is the mad cry of vengeance,
The finality that knows no succor.
These gifts She brings to you.
Bring no gold or sweetest wine to Her altars.
Salute Her instead with blood and ash.

Bring Her barbed wire, canisters of gas,

Wood for kindling witches.

Bring Her that which fuels your devotions.

That on which your sacred halls are built.

Bring Her the heart pierced by anguish,

The bodies of children slaughtered by the young.

Do not lie in the face of Inanna.

Do not spit in the face of Inanna.

Your temples and schools and holy places stand empty.

So bring Her what you truly revere.

Pile high your altars with the shit of your choices.

And when She opens Her mouth to speak,

The silence will destroy you.

From the abyss, Inanna beckons.

Keeper of the *Me*
Raven Kaldera

You came into the hall of Enki,
The inventor, the clever one,
But you were cleverer still.

For Enki created the *Me*,
The words of power that rule all,
Instruct all, build civilization.
Did you envy him, O Queen of Heaven?
Did you, beautiful and charming, see him
Bent nebbishly over his altar,
Locked to his work like a lover,
In the age-old dance of Making.
He was no handsome one, he had no charm.
Yet this he could do. Did you envy him,
O radiant splendor of life,
Darling of heaven?

Supreme in power, Inanna of Heaven and Earth,
Whose mouth rains sparkles of lightning over the land,
Mistress of beasts, given the gods' life-spirits by An,
By An given the unfailing Word
To speak at his fateful command:
Who can fathom your glory?

You swept into his hall like the prom queen
Paying a visit to the class nerd, and like
That one, he could only be glad to see you.
Drink poured—you saw to it—and he drowned
His wisdom in your beauty, in the hope of
Something more. You asked, he gave,
His eyes on your cleavage. You asked, he gave,
His eyes on your bared thigh. You asked,

He gave all to you without thinking,
The scent of your musk in his eyes,
The rose of your flesh across the table.
Then you left him wanting, your hands
Full of the *Me* that were his greatest creation.

Jeweled and crowned with life,
In your hand are the guardian spirits of the Seven Gods,
And you yourself guard and protect the guardian spirits,
You have taken them up and tied them to your hands,
Have gathered them in and pressed them to your breast.

When the booze wore off and the pale day dawned
And the pillow beneath his clutch proved to be
No more than that, he was enraged. Every creature
He had made, he flung at you
To regain all that he had lost. But you had aid,
You commanded loyalty with your beauty
And your maidservant, your warrior girl fended
All of them off to ensure your escape.

Like a bird you scavenge the land.
Like a charging storm you charge,
Like a roaring storm you roar,
You thunder in thunder,
Snort in rampaging winds.
Your feet are continually restless.
Carrying your harp of sighs,
You breathe out the music of mourning.

And triumphant you return, O Inanna,
The *Me* like jewels in your crown.
Yet one was left that he did not give away;
One that one day he would use
Out of his own generosity

To free you from your dark imprisonment,
Even though he might have done otherwise.
What generosity did you learn from this, Inanna?
What pricked you as you marched up
From your sister's realm, flanked by demons
And by the ones who freed you, his children—
Did it run through your mind that if
You had had your way, stripped him
Of all that was his, of all that he had done
You would still hang on a hook in the Underworld
Decorating the still abyss of your sister's throne?
You are the lesson that no one wants to hear:
You are the road that all prom queens must walk
Sooner or later, whether they will or no.

You came into the hall of Enki,
The inventor, the clever one,
But though you were cleverer still,
The rod of your wisdom was broken
On Irkalla's dusty stairs
And to whom, now, do you owe your life,
Radiant One,
Beloved of Heaven and Earth.

And so we journey from the realm of light, through the shadows, into the realm of darkness. We move from Inanna, Queen of Heaven to Ereshkigal, Queen of the Great Below. May They both be praised.

Prayer to Ereshkigal
Kira R.

Queen of the Nether realms,
Shelter of the battered soul,
Protectress of the dead
Be Thou praised.

Queen of Deepest Earth,
Bringer of Solace,
You offer a place of peace
To the dead:
To the warrior dead
To the aged dead
To the infant dead
To the youthful dead
To the weeping dead
To the rejoicing dead
You Whose doors welcome all those
coming from the place of Life,
Be Thou honored.

Bone Lady, Weeping Queen,
Wearing warrior-marks of grief naked upon Your regal cheeks,
No sorrow goes unnoticed by Your keenness.
You weep for the child dead in the womb.
You weep for the warrior, sacrificed on the field of battle.
You weep for those left behind in the hands of grief.
Oh Shelter of our Souls, be Thou comforted.

I honor the Queen of Irkalla.
I honor the magnificent Queen.
I bow my head to Ereshkigal
Queen of the Great Below.
Be She ever praised!

Hymn to Ereshkigal I

Rebecca Buchanan

Eres Ki Gala
Dark-haired Queen of Irkalla
Who sleeps naked amid the bones
In her palace of brilliant blue

Eres Ki Gala
Black-haired Queen of Irkalla
Elder sister of tempestuous Inanna
Who defends her rightful realm with strength and cunning

Eres Ki Gala
Night-haired Queen of Irkalla
Who suckles lion cubs at her breasts
And lets loose the treasures of the earth

Eres Ki Gala
Fearsome
Awe-full
Queen of Irkalla

Erishkegal, Goddess of the Last Resort
Elizabeth Barette

When the Heavens and the Earth had been created,
And all the spheres of influence claimed but one,
There remained the Underworld in need of mastery.
"What a nasty job," said Enki. "No one wants it!"
With that, he discarded the key to the lapis palace.
"I'll do it," said Erishkegal.
And so she did.

When the manners of men and women had been made,
And Inanna had established the arts of love,
Nergal went and invented rape.
"What a nasty god," said Inanna. "No one wants him!"
So she cast him out of Heaven.
"I'll civilize him," said Erishkegal.
And so she did.

When the letters and words had all been designed,
And Nebo set them down with stylus and clay
He discovered that he had accidentally invented stagnation.
"What a nasty problem," said Nebo.
"No one knows what to do about it!"
Moaning, he buried his face in his hands.
"I'll fix it," said Erishkegal.
And so she did.

She broke Nebo's tablet over his hard head,
Thus inventing chaos.
The other goddesses and gods
May not like Erishkegal much ...
But they'd be lost without her.

Hymn to Ereshkigal II

Rebecca Buchanan

Great Lady Under the Earth
Mistress of Irkalla
When Nergal stormed your realm
      daring to claim it for his own
You lay with him
In your palace of lapis and bone
      and so won his heart:

Queen of Kur
      soon
      you will own my heart
      too

Katabasis
J.D.

In the darkness
my heartbeat echoes,
then is silent.

I stand before the first gate.
Feathers and dust
fall from my fingers.
I pick up my gifts.
There is doubt behind me,
but none before me
as I nod to the gatekeeper.

He says, "You must."
I give him my ears.
I step inside.

Here there is a tightrope walk
of sinew. I make my
way across. I cannot hear
the wind howling.

I stand before the second gate
and the gatekeeper says, "You must."
I give him my throat.
I step inside.

This path is a maze
through holes, through marrow.
I cannot scream.

I stand before the third gate
and the gatekeeper says, "You must."

I give him my tongue.
I step inside.

This path is a whirlwind of dust.
Though it fills my mouth,
I cannot taste it.

I stand before the fourth gate
and the gatekeeper says, "You must."
I give him my nose.
I step inside.

Here there are bodies
of every shape and stage of decay,
rotting. I cannot
smell the flesh.

I stand before the fifth gate
and the gatekeeper says, "You must."
I give him my skin.
I step inside.

Here there are coals,
awkward and shifting
under my feet. They may be
hot or sharp. I cannot
tell; I cannot feel them.

I stand before the sixth gate
and the gatekeeper says, "You must."
I give him my eyes.
I step inside.

This is a void.
The unknown, to be crossed.

There is darkness I cannot see.

I stand before the seventh gate
and the gatekeeper says, "You must."
I give him my heart.
He places it in a jar
and hands it back to me.
I step inside.

Here there is a throne.
Here there is a table
adorned with dust.
Here there are servants
adorned with feathers.

My lady Dark,
my dear Ereshkigal,
sits on her throne.

I kneel before her.

"Lady, though you have
come to me a hundred times
on wings and whispers,
I come to you now.
I will go where you send me
only set me on the path.
I will say what you will me
only give me the words.
I will do as you bid me
only show me a plan."

I laid my head
in the dust at her feet
and I waited.

"Do you know of whom
you ask this?"
she says, finally.

"I ask it of you, my Lady,
Ereshkigal called Irkalla,
Queen of the Land Below,
wife of Nergal,
master of Namtar,
who once knew the sky
and was brought below,
who is now the mistress of bones,
the ruler of the lands
of dust and feathers,
who sits in judgment
of the gods below,
who keeps the dead
and turns the seasons
and ends all things."

I stand before her throne.
I offer her the first jar.
She opens the lid
and tastes the honey.
Her dark lips smile.

I offer her the second jar.
She opens the lid
and tastes the tears.
Her dark eyes close.

I offer her the third jar.
She opens the lid
and studies my heart.
Her dark face nods.

I watch my heart crumble
to dust in her hands.
I taste ash.
I feel my muscles rotting,
my blood drying,
bones bared.

I whisper "Remake me,"
through cracked lips.

She nods.

"I was waiting for that."
And then her hand
is on my head.
And then my bones
are clothed in sinew.
And then my muscles
are clothed in skin.
And then my body
is clothed in feathers.

She bids me "Stand."
I do.
She bids me "Go."
And though I do not understand,
I turn from her.

"Put your path before me,
Lady," I beg.

Then I fly up
through the seventh and the sixth gate
through the fifth and the fourth gate
through the third and the second gate

through the first gate.

When I turn and look,
the gates have never been there.

In one hand, I hold dust.
It is not the same as that I left with.
In the other, I hold feathers.
It is not the same as those I left with.
In my chest, I hold my heart.
It is not the same as the one I left with.

I close my eyes and I can
see her just

Underground
Courtney Righter (Sister Dea Phoebe)

Take away my accomplishments
I still have my voice
Take away my voice
I still have my will.
Take away my will
I still have my Name.
Take away my voice, my will, my name
And I still have my self.
Take away my self
Rend me to the bones
Hang me to rot, to decompose
Let the flesh fall from my bones
Everything I am sloughing away like it never was
And I will still have a foundation
On which to rebuild.

II.
I stand at the Gates of the Unknown
Having heard the call from deep within.
Knowing not whether these wandering paths lead
To light
Or darkness
Destruction
Or redemption.
In my mind, in my heart, in my bones
I hear the deepening rumble
Of a Loud Thundering Storm.

III.
Queen of Heaven and of Earth
When You made those first steps
To the Great Below

Did You know that when
Everything was stripped away
The core would remain
To give fiery rebirth to Yourself,
A Phoenix, Triumphant
Desiring all love
All the world
Or where those first steps into the endless dark
Taken in fearful faith?

Invocation to Ereshkigal

First published in Pagan Book of Hours *by the Order of the Horae
Asphodel Press, 2006. Used with permission.*

Lady of Irkalla, Lady of the Darkness,
Widow of Gugulanna, the Great Bull of Heaven,
Widow of Nergal, conqueror of hubris,
Who drinks water with the Annunaki,
Who eats dust and clay for bread, who drinks river-mud for beer,
Who weeps for the young men forced to abandon their sweethearts,
Who weeps for the girls wrenched from their lovers' laps,
Who weeps for the infant child, expelled before its time,
We hail you in your mourning.
Mistress of the Seven Gates
Guarded by Neti, Gatekeeper of the Underworld
Who answers only to Ereshkigal,
We hail you in your sorrow.
Lady who holds the water-gift, the river in its fullness,
Lady who holds the grain-gift, the fields in their fullness,
Lady who held the Queen of Heaven in her arrogance,
Hung her on the wall like a piece of meat,
Ransomed only by the tears
Of those neither male nor female,
And then sent her back only to have
Her husband instead, to decorate your throne,
May we all learn the wisdom of the Kurgarra and Galatur!
May we learn to weep for Death
And feel compassion for even that which we fear,
For this, too, is your painful lesson.
Lady of Irkalla, help us to move beyond ourselves
And our fears, and see all endings with new eyes.

Naked And Bowed Low

Janet Munin

In The Descent of Inanna, after going through the seven gates of the underworld and losing a piece of her regalia at each one, Inanna is said to enter the throne room of Ereshkigal "naked and bowed low". I wanted to take the phrase and give it a different meaning.

I entered the throne room naked and bowed low
Understand, you who listen
I did not say broken
I did not say tortured or beaten or shamed
I entered unencumbered
I entered in humility and gratitude
I entered in awe and adoration
I laid my head in the lap of the Goddess
I bared my throat to the Bitch of the Great Below
I surrendered myself to the Queen of Irkalla
For the knife edge of Her mercy is my salvation
And in Her fierce love I embrace eternity

Part II
Prayers To Other
Sumerian Deities

Invocation to Enki

First published in Pagan Book of Hours *by the Order of the Horae*
Asphodel Press, 2006. Used with permission.

Enki is the Sumerian God of creation (the 'ki' in His name means 'earth')
and intellect. Because of His quick and cunning work in creating the galatur and
kurgarra, Inanna was able to be freed from the Underworld.

Hear now the words of Enki the Great, Lord of Sweet waters!
"My father, the king of the universe, brought me into existence.
My ancestor, the king of all the lands,
Gathered together all the, *me,*
Placed the *me* in my hand.
From the Ekur, the house of Enlil,
I brought craftsmanship to my Abzu of Eridu.
I am the fecund seed engendered by the great wild ox,
I am the first born son of An,
I am the hurricane who goes forth out of the great below,
I am the gugal of the chieftains,
I am the father of all the lands,
I am the elder brother of the gods,
I am he who brings full prosperity,
I am the record keeper of heaven and earth,
I am he who directs justice with the king An on An's dais.
At my command the stalls have been built,
The sheepfolds have been enclosed,
When I approached heaven
A rain of prosperity poured down from heaven,
When I approached the earth, there was a high flood,
When I approached its green meadows,
The heaps and mounds were piled up at my word."
Hail Enki, Lord of Sweet Waters,
Creator of the *me!*

Stonebreaker: A Call To Gugulanna, The Bull Of Heaven
Lee Harrington

Gugulanna was Ereshkigal's first Husband. He was sent by Inanna to take vengeance on Gilgamesh, who dismembered Him. In many accounts of Inanna's descent, Her stated reason for going to visit Her sister is to offer condolences for His death.

We each need a first to open us up to our potential, to pave the way for future tales, to shake us from our comfort zones. In Gugalanna, Ereshkigal found that first husband, the Bull of Heaven, who came to Kur and paved the way for her own future, the Mistress of the shadowed lands of the dead and more, she who was strong enough to take those lands when no others would and yet not strong enough to love or cry fully.

This call to Gugalanna is a call to find a breaker of stones in your own life. Not to be taken lightly, this call asks for someone to shake us from our comfort zones, slay our dragons, show us a mirror to our potential and find us a pathway to our own road through life. Be mindful that this may take many forms, and can manifest in astral aide, internal dialogue, or an actual individual who will come temporarily into our lives and shake our world or manifest into this role then leave, not always in the easiest way. For strongest calling force, consider doing this in a dark mirror, in a mirror in a darkened room, or under the auspices of the new moon.

Monster in my bones
Beloved of my first tears
I hear you breaking stones
I hear you breaking stones
In my heart

Gugalanna in my bones
Bull of Heaven in Kur
I claim the fear and woes
I claim the fear and woes
In my heart

I battle monsters
Each day
I battle you my sweet
Each day
I battle my reflection
Each day
In the shadowed lands of Kur

Monster in my bones
Beloved of my first tears
I hear you breaking stones
I hear you breaking stones
In my heart

To Stay A Seventh Day: Nergal Sings To Ereshkigal
Lee Harrington

Nergal (or Nirgal) is a Sumerian deity of war, associated in part with the power of the Sun. He is Ereshkigal's Husband and with Her, presides over the Underworld.

Touch me, my love, and lie with me
Touch me, my love, and be my mate
Six days shall we lay, my love
And on the Seventh I shall not flee

Long ago, my love, my father came here
Long ago, my father and mother came here
My father your father's first born
And the man that made your father shed tears

You could not come to the feast. my love
You could not be there in the flesh
So I knew not the shame I did, my love
And I would not bow before your minister

Namtar whose name is Fate saw me
Namtar whose name is Fate told you, my love
He took this shame back to your ears
And I knew I would have to make amends

I went to your brother Ea to ask
I went to your twin of Magic born in tears
His laughter erupted as I told him my folly
And he shook his head at my pride

He had me make a throne of sacred woods
He had me heed how not to stay seven days
To eat nothing, take nothing, leave nothing
And warned me never to lie with you

So with his blessing I made a throne
So with his blessing I descended the stairs
I asked Namtar to admit me at the gate
And he shook his head at my pride

I brought you gifts to make amends
I brought you gifts to show you my power
For I am the god of War and Pestilence
And I thought to stand sovereign before you

For I am a Prince born of Enlil and Ninlil
For I am the Justice of the Gods on Earth
So I stood before your sovereign throne
And turned away your hospitality, my love

You took from me the throne my love
You took from me my loneliness
As I sat with you and talked, my love
And found in your skin my equal and more

I gave in to my heart's desire, my love
I gave in to you and did what men and women do
We embraced each other, my love
And went passionately to bed

We lay there, you, my Queen, and I
We lay there for a first and second day
Together our flesh and sweat mingling
And our moans and laughter echoed loud

Queen of the Underworld, you took me in
Queen of my heart, you conquered me
We lay there for a third day
And our hearts sung out to every shadow

My love, you opened up to my lust
My love, you opened up to my joy
In the land of the Dead, Justice and Memory
And we lay there for a fourth day

We found in each other a mirror
We found a way to abandon loneliness
We lay there for a fifth day
And acknowledged each other's strength and love

Together we lay for a sixth day
Together we whispered and smiled
Finding strength in each other's skin
And fell asleep spent in each other's arms

Waking before you my love
Waking before you in the dark I sat
Remembering what Ea had told me
And became afraid of staying forever at your side

I crept out on swift and silent feet
I crept out like the lurking death I spread
Fleeing into the night I fled from your bed
And ascended the stairway back to heaven

Namtar came to you, my love
Namtar came and told you of my folly
Your faithful vizier came to you as you woke
And your rage shook the earth above and below

They say you cried out aloud grievously
They say you fell from your throne
Straightened up from the ground and wept
And tears flowed down both your cheeks

But I could hear nothing of it
But I could think of nothing but my fear
I was afraid of giving in to love and life
And could not believe I had found both below

In short time Namtar came to the heavens
In short time he brought your words to us
That you were a woman of complexities and power
And I came to the hall to hear what he had to say

I heard him speak of your childhood, my love
I heard him speak of your loneliness below
Of your power as Queen of the Underworld
And your rage in my behavior for how I left

The Gods all then looked to me
The Gods all shook their head at my folly
Oh Nergal, they sighed and pitied me
And each pressed the case for and against you

Finally I sat alone with my thoughts
Finally I sat and thought of you, my love
Six days and nights I conjured in my mind
And remembered just what it was that I had left

I remembered your smile and moans
I remembered the way I felt at your side
Then sat and tore my hair knowing I needed you
And cried at my pride and arrogance

Twice now I had insulted you
Twice now I had shamed myself
I did not know that you had sent Namtar
And did not know he took those tears back to you

I caught myself in a mirror, my love
I caught myself and saw my soul for a moment
In that moment I saw what you had seen in me
And I knew I could be all you saw and loved

Descending the stairs I let go of my folly
Descending the stairs I let go of my pride
Namtar stopped, almost smiled, as I passed
And allowed me into your chamber unannounced

For by Dakuni what is above is below
For by Dakuni our love will echo on every plane
Oh my love, forgive me and love me again
And together we will soar

Let me be your king at your side
Let me support you in your greatness
For you have shown me the worst I could be
And you will always show me the best I am

Touch me, my love, and lie with me
Touch me, my love, and be my mate
Six days shall we lay my love
And on the Seventh I shall not flee

Touch me, my love, and lie with me
Touch me, my love, for a first and second day
As our flesh and sweat mingle together
And our moans and laughter echo out loud

Touch me, my love, and lie with me
Touch me as you conquer my heart
We will lay here for a third day
And our hearts will sing to every shadow

Touch me, my love, and lie with me
Touch me and open my lust and my joy
In the land of the Dead, Justice and Memory
And we will lay here for a fourth day

Touch me, my love, and lie with me
Touch me as we both abandon loneliness
We will lie here for a fifth day
And acknowledge each other's strength and love

Touch me, my love, and lie with me
Touch me and whisper and smile
Find strength in my skin as I find it in yours
And we sleep spent in each others arms

Touch me, my love, and lie with me
Touch me my love and be my mate
Six days have passed as we lay my love
And on the Seventh I did not flee

Invocation to Dumuzi

First published in Pagan Book of Hours *by First Kingdom Church of Asphodel,* *(2006). MA: Asphodel Press. Used with permission.*

Hail, Lord of the flocks and herds
Who is slaughtered that we may live.
Hail, sacred king of Babylon
Who gives his life for Inanna's freedom
And for Ereshkigal's hunger.
Hail, reluctant one who goes unwillingly
To the sacrifice, as many of us do,
Yet who learns the beauty and dignity
Of the path of being an offering.

It is the nature of sacrifice
To be difficult.
If it was easy to throw away,
It was no sacrifice.
If you did not miss it
It was no sacrifice.
If it was not the best you could give
It was no sacrifice.
If it was not agonizing to choose,
It was no sacrifice.
If it did not make you waver at least once in your choice,
It was no sacrifice.
If it did not make you weep,
It was no sacrifice.

Ninshubur

Raven Kaldera

Ninshubur is a Warrior Goddess and Inanna's devoted friend and servant. She keeps vigil as Inanna makes Her descent into the Underworld.

I am the hawk poised on the wrist of my Queen,
Silent, hooded, waiting to be released
Into the sky where I kill for her,
Bring her back gifts of the heads of her enemies.

I am the hound tensed at the heel of my Queen,
Patient, vigilant, waiting to be commanded
To the throats of those who would threaten her,
And may they fall before me like chaff!

I am the dove perched on the shoulder of my Queen,
Cheerful, cooing, waiting to be cast
Into the winds with the message to her paramours,
Bearing their wistful replies safely to her hand.

I am the monkey curled at the feet of my Queen,
Nimble, affectionate, fetching this and that
With antics to turn sorrow to joy, and comfort
When it is needed, with the press of my small body.

I am a flower of service
Opened to your hand, O Inanna.
Only with your plucking am I given differentiation,
Only with your need am I given purpose,
Only with the inhalation of your breath
To judge my quality—only by this
Am I made Ninshubur, Inanna's woman,
And not some faceless servant in the crowd.

Would you have me be soft
And dress your hair, drape you in colors
For your next lover's bedding, redden your nails
And speculate with you on their performance,
My laughter ringing sweet to lift your heart?
This I can do.

Would you have me be hard
And stand behind you armed and armored,
Grim of visage that none may insult you,
Fighting a hundred demons for you,
My blade leaping in your protection?
This also I can do.

Would you have me bend like the willow,
Defer to you, take your advice,
Your judgment as mine, my strings yours to pull,
Dancing for you like a child's puppet,
Taking joy in your every whim?
This also I can do.

Would you have me strong as iron,
Waiting in the dust for you by Irkalla's passage,
Screaming at the gates of the mighty
For your rescue, untiring and impassioned,
Until the Gods give way before me for your aid?
This also I can do.

I will do all this
And ask nothing more of you
Than your regard, your smile of pleasure,
And the knowledge that I ease the earthly life
Of the Queen of Heaven—what greater honor?

Depend on me

As on the mountain's stone
To change like the springtime winds
Into whatever shape you need,
Until you need another.
I am your shadow, O Inanna,
As true service shadows true power,
Linked at the heel, I move behind you,
Every footprint you leave in the sand
Shows my eternal devotion at your back.

Neti

Raven Kaldera

Neti is the gatekeeper of Irkalla and Ereshkigal's chief servant.

The stones are worn down
Before the great gates of Irkalla
Where I keep my watch, night after night.
My tread has worn them smooth, my feet
With one goal only: to guard my Queen
From what part of the tide I can yet hold back.

My Queen, I watch the haggard souls
Come through this gate at your command,
Swarm at your throne, demand of you
Comfort, wisdom, judgment, harshness,
All that Life did not give them, this
They expect of you. And you give,
And give, until you are emptied
And hollow of eye. You take them into you,
Rebirth them again, to move on to new lives
Where they can rejoice in the Sun
And curse your name again.

I see your pain.
I see you weep and moan, your belly
Filled with grief, you flail alone
On the cold flagstones before your throne,
Dead men's castoffs clutched about you.
I would take from you these burdens,
O Ereshkigal, yet it cannot be done.
You must walk this path, for someone
Must be the Dark One, and not I. I can only
Weep in my heart for you, and keep my watch
And turn away the foolish, the unworthy

That you might be relieved of one small
Percentage of sorrow. My shoulders are bowed
With the weight of centuries, but it is nothing
To your road. How can I not be loyal
To the end, with your example before me?
O Queen of Death, I will never forsake you.

I am ugly, yet you find beauty in my constancy,
In my cold heart. You share muddy water with me
When those of the upper world drink wine,
And I give you always the clearest part.
I share your darkness, without complaint,
With red-eyed demons that cut the air
To dusty ribbons. The devourers at fine tables
Bright in the upper world, they laugh at us,
At our poverty. They do not understand.
To serve in luxury is easy. To serve in want,
In strife, in the tear-streaked dogged exhaustion of
Both master and man, that is where honor is forged.
To find one cup of comfort in the wilderness
And offer it up, that is worth true pride.

Yet still the fools come, to steal what you
Give freely to each shattered ghost.
I look upon them with cold eyes
And deny them entrance to smirk at our tatters.
Begone, you laughing vicious birds
Else I might pluck your glittering plumage
And leave your bones scattered about
The worn stones of my blurred gate.
O my Queen of all the black and howling winds,
I would die a hundred deaths before
I would ever let them see your pain.

For Tiamatu

Dee Bellwether

Tiamat is the great dragon goddess of primordial waters from whose body the world was created.

Gurgling
Clicking
Vomiting
Vaginal Voidal Voiceless Vacuum
Your Language is Not
Your Light is UnLight
You Are The Lady Who Is Nothing
Queen of Unmaking
Twisting Serpent of UnKnowledge
UnMake Me in Your Image
Your every nuance of Emptiness
Entwines Existence
Defining 'Ness
All That Is
By All That Is Not
Never Was
And Never Shall Be.

Invocation to Tiamat

First published in Pagan Book of Hours *by the Order of the Horae*
Asphodel Press, 2006. Used with permission.

Mother of Dragons
Mother of Serpents
Sea-green goddess
Ocean's floor become fertile earth
Spiral of wave become wave of mountain
Arching foam become arch of sky
Sea of Aether that swirls
Deep within our minds
From the waters we came
From the waters we are born
To the waters we shall return
For our rebirths.
You whose body is the world
Who is all around us
Sacrificed in order to become
Omniscient
Mother of Dragons
Mother of Serpents
Lead us onward through the tides
Of our uncertain lives.

(If you would use this invocation in a ritual: On a sea green cloth place a large chalice of salt water, strings of pearls and beads in a spiral pattern like a whirlpool, and figures of dragons and sea serpents. The invocation should be read, then each pours water on themselves.

Allow yourself to experience conflicting and turbulent emotions that you would otherwise avoid. Each person stands forth and speaks of themselves as an emotion, saying, "I am happiness" or "I am sorrow".

Then one person who has been chosen to do the work of the ritual takes a sword and walks around the circle, miming slaying each person, who falls to the ground, saying, "Die, and become one with the earth." All lay on their backs with hands joined, heads facing inward, and each visualizes themself as part of the earth, and they speak out what part of the earth they and their emotion have become—"I who was joy am now rivers!" "I who was anger am now desert." "I who was wonder am now mountain ranges!" and so on.

End in a chant: Aiyu Tiamat Tiamat Tiamat Your body all around.)

Tiamat Chant
Kira R.

I am Tiamat
From Me were you born
in that time the world forgot.

I am Dragon Goddess spinning
The end of the cosmos
Back to the beginning.

It may seem strange to include prayers to Lilith in a Sumerian devotional but surprisingly, some of the oldest known references to Lilith occur in Inanna's canon. Inanna had a sacred Tree, the Huluppu-Tree. She nurtured and cared for this tree and the surviving prayer cycles state that "the dark maid Lilith built her home in the trunk." (Weinstein, p. 6). Eventually, when Gilgamesh came to drive out the other creatures (a serpent and great bird) that also resided in the Tree, Lilith smashed her home and fled to "wild, uninhabited places." (Weinstein, p. 9). From this Tree, Inanna then carved Her throne.

For Lilith
Elizabeth Vongvisith

I loved you, dweller in the *huluppu* tree,
before the burden of Sigyn's arms
became my arms' glad burden too.

O thou, proud, crowned and erect,
who rode Adam like a Harley,
revving his engine between your legs.

Child-snatcher, blood drinker,
winged spirit of the city, wielder
of the sacred, telling rod and ring—

Lilith darkest, sweet flower
in that eternal night-robed garden
of sensual, irresistible earthly delight.

Those sober-clad men, shrinking
at your seductive might, Lady,
underneath their prayer shawls—

they called you demoness and scribed
chalk circles over babies' cradles.
I feel no sympathy for them,

since my own womb has borne
nothing but death, and I loved you
even after you kidnapped its fruit

and gorged yourself on the flesh
of my flesh, bloodstained teeth showing
as you smirked at me with perfect delight.

I would bedeck you with night-jasmine,
myrrhs and sweet aloes, and paint your lips
with the nectar that runs down my thighs.

I would embrace you, death-bringer,
owl-woman, and watch my fist vanish
all the way into your ever-hungry cunt.

I would bare my naked throat to you,
vampire bitch, raptor of the bedchamber—
were it not already promised to another.

O thou terrible, awesome Mother of Night,
sister of feathers and teeth and breasts,
I write this love song for you

because I understand now, Lady,
how the deepest desires of my heart
have always been tinged with your shadow.

Hands Outstretched
Anya Kless

If only there had been no Adam.
If only it had remained a woman and her God
in Paradise.

Did she seduce Him, as they say,
to learn the secret name?
Or did He give it freely,
in a moment of terrible compassion?

"This is your out."

Submission or exile
Man's subject or God's rival

She laughed as the tears fell,
stunned by His ingenuity
His generosity
His cruelty

It was an easy choice.

After all, what woman could lie beneath a man
after knowing God?

She spoke the name.
Her wings sprouted like black cancer.
She did not look back as she cleared the walls.
She found the desert and her demons.
Her pain festered, her rage became eternal.

Did she discover her serpent form
And slither back into Eden for revenge?

Or did He give it to her,
to become the sacred adversary,
to take up the terrible mantle of all taboos?

Hail the Desert Queen
Hail She Who Will Not Be Tamed
Hail the Annihilating Feminine

Hail Lilith, Mother of Demons
Hail She, Beloved of Yahweh

Part III
Rituals
To Inanna
And Ereshkigal

Ecstatic Darkness
Rev. Galina Krasskova

When I initially began studying for the priesthood in the Fellowship of Isis, I was fortunate enough to have the guidance of an incredibly creative Lyceum in NYC. Many of the women there excelled in the arts of music, drama, singing and dance. It was only natural then, that one of the Goddesses most often invoked in our rituals was the Goddess Inanna, for to us She symbolized ecstatic celebration and ecstatic creativity. What's more, the story of Her descent into the Underworld was the primary paradigm of our initiation rituals. Rebirth came through Inanna.

For all of that, I never particularly liked this Goddess. She evoked no great feeling in me, there was no special connection there. I never felt any antipathy toward Her, but She was a "pretty" Goddess with little other function than that of sex and decoration. When She was spoken of, it was usually in the context of extolling her bold sexuality and Her sacred marriage with the God Dumuzi. It held little appeal despite what I was also reading about the enormity of Her descent. The prodigious error of my assumptions was something I never realized until many years later. First, I too had to meet Ereshkigal.

Ereshkigal. Even the name speaks of beauty to me, a beauty born of loneliness, pain and a quiet enduring strength like that of the phoenix fighting its way forth from the ashes of its own immolation. It is a beauty born not of joy but of suffering and resolution within the self. So many images come to mind when I whisper that name. She is delicate and fragile in Her beauty yet at the same time, terrible and ravenous. Her grief and rage may shatter worlds and yet hold the key to healing of the heart. More than any other Goddess I had encountered up to that point, She understood grief and pain and the terrible soul-twisting loneliness of being a woman unadorned and forgotten.

Leave Inanna to the beautiful, the graceful, those blessed to be what our culture considers both feminine and pretty (so I told myself). I will offer libation to Ereshkigal. I will bring to Her my hurt, my bitterness, my dull rooted rage and longing and know that I will not be turned away with faux words of comfort: "You are just too intense," or "If only you would fix your hair just so, if only you would wear a bit of make-up, smile more and then..." and then you will be loved. No, such facades serve not this Goddess of darkness. From Her I learned that there is beauty in a blade equal to that of the delicate blossoms most women seek to be. From Her I learned to shriek my pain to the heavens, to give it voice, to own my anger and by owning create the change I wished to see in my life. I learned to rest in the darkness and find in the endless change it brings a peculiar peace of being. I learned that power comes from learning to stand alone and strong, compassion from being willing to reach out to another in pain, despite old agonies. All facades, all barriers all neatly delineated zones of comfort disintegrated in the face of this Goddess leaving only the simple reality of being. And of healing. I stood naked in the halls of Ereshkigal. And I thrived.

It was a year after founding my own Lyceum that I first invoked Her and oh, I thought my heart would break. She came with the piercing, penetrating force of a blade silently slipped between the ribs in darkness. She came in a flood of grief and bitterness that forced me to crumple to the floor under its weight. And as I wept, opening the best I could to experience the grace of this Goddess, to give voice if possible to Her wisdom I felt the pain lessen and She embraced me. Sitting in the darkness of my temple, with only a single candle's flame for illumination, I felt myself cradled in the arms of Ereshkigal. And in the words She whispered it was as though a treasure box of wisdom and magic had been opened for my eager fingers to peruse. She did not force Her presence but when invited came with undeniable frankness and power. She did not demand that discomfort and anger be hidden under a pleasant mask of meaningless platitudes, rather She reflected all the grief and rage the world had ever held. One need not be "pretty" with Ereshkigal. But one had best be true. I began to work with Ereshkigal, quietly inviting Her to be my teacher in the path of my own healing.

Sadly, it seemed even then that She stood a silent second to Her sister Inanna. Two incidents stand out strongly in my mind: The first occurred in a public ritual hosted by a fairly popular study group and student circle. During the ritual, a meditation was done in which attendees went on a pathworking to find their Patron Goddess. One woman approached the "teacher" after the ritual and told her that she had had a very powerful experience with Ereshkigal, detailing it in some depth. The teacher's response: "We don't work with Goddesses like that." (Needless to say I spoke with the girl afterwards myself!). The second was something that my co-priest said in passing, after meditating on Ereshkigal: "When I think on Ereshkigal, I see a bag lady forced to pick through garbage, to pick through things discarded for her treasures because no one ever brings her gifts directly."

Ereshkigal then, is a Goddess of the neglected, the cast-off, the unwanted, the discarded and disavowed. She is the Goddess for those who know what it is like to be unloved, uprooted, caught in the conflict between strength and passion, or fear and hate. She is the ever infertile mother whose children are beyond number. She is a Goddess who can look at all of these things we have learned to call ugly, to treat with shame, to hide away and Her only response is acceptance. They do not repulse as we could never repulse. They simply are. Ereshkigal embraces all of these things and from them opens the door to immense strength. They are the bricks with which the road is built that leads us out of Her abyss.

Some believe that Inanna and Ereshkigal are the same Goddess, but I have never found it to be so. Rather, Ereshkigal mirrors back to Inanna all the things that Inanna must face and overcome. Ereshkigal is the challenger and always the victor in an ever ongoing battle against pride and ego. Inanna met the face of Her sister with joy and there is something very potent in that. Inanna's own journey is very much bracketed by the most ancient Goddesses of wisdom and deepest, darkest earth: She gains Her throne by meeting Lilith. She gains Herself by surrendering to Ereshkigal. If a Goddess like Inanna could see in the dark realm of Her sister, something beyond price, a prize of the self worth any struggle, certainly we can do the same.

Dark Moon Rite Of Ereshkigal

Rev. Galina Krasskova

In the beginning, smudge everyone with copal incense. Cast the circle in whatever way your circle normally does, preferably with chanting to raise energy.

Call the elementals invoking the Galla of the East, Galla of the South, etc. In the center for the spirit, invoke Ereshkigal's consort Nergal. The Galla are beings of Ereshkigal's realm, and their primary function is serving their Goddess.

The Altar: The cloth should be black. The candles should be black or dark purple. Starkness is the key here however as many of the following items should be placed thereon:

Bones and skulls
Black heart made of stone
Obsidian, garnet, hematite, black crystals
Pomegranates
Black feathers
A chalice of water and few drops of Dark Moon Goddess oil
Gargoyles, gryphons and dragons
A Medusa Image
Black vase of black or red roses, lotus pods, and irises
Serpent Goddess (Cretan or Mycenaean)
Wormwood
A cauldron
A dagger
Wands
Cowrie shells

Anything else that reminds you of Her. An image of Her is always welcome; just be sure that She approves. All references to Inanna in the temple or sacred space should be removed or covered up.

Quarter Invocations:

East

As I look to the East,
I call upon the Dreaded Galla
Who guard the Hellgates of the East.
Come fast, come strong,
Come with the swiftness of the wind.
Hear our call, we cry out to you.
Sear into our minds the price of cowardly silence,
All the trouble a too-loose tongue can cause.
Gorge yourself on all the debris
Unwittingly heaped upon us
By the outside world of the mundane.
Feast upon all that would impede
Our communion with Thy Queen.
May your razor-sharp talons tear away
Every trace of the masks and shrouds of protection
We cast about ourselves
While leaving our true essences intact and pure.
May we look upon your terrible face
And mourn your loss of flight as you wallow
In the mire of all the darkness of the world.
May our river of tears wash away
All the grime and the dirt
Cloaking the precious light you have long ago lost.
Come partake of the incense, nature's sweet perfume,
Heaven to lonely nostrils hungering
For the scent of just one rose.
Under your guidance, may we realize how dear
Our connection to Deity truly is
And the power of our words,
Our voices, our songs, our breath.
May you inspire us to open our minds and hearts
To all the Gods' and Goddesses' glory
And give resounding testaments of thanks and praise

To all their blessed names.
O Dread Eastern Galla,
Steal away from thy abyss and with us be joined,
As we humbly say hail and welcome.

South:
As I look to the South,
I call upon the dreaded Galla of the South,
Guardians of the sacred Hellfire and the Southern Gates.
Come fast, come strong,
Come with the heat of a thousand blazing suns
Shining forth proud in all their dazzling glory.
Burn into our minds the folly of giving up our willfire
For what we perceive to be a greater treasure.
For all the riches and love of others in the world
Are but worthless trinkets if to our own selves we are untrue.
You of immense strength,
Break the chains of uncertainty and self doubt
We wrap about ourselves.
Destroy with thy flame all our thoughts
Of unworthiness and weakness.
For while we may have limits, Deity has none,
And with Them by our side,
All roads are well lit and open.
O Abominable Ones, we cry for your existence
In a realm of darkness no light can shatter
Save the radiance of thy Queen.
Come, be with us in circle,
Be driven as a moth is to a flame
To those that welcome you for all you are.
Under your guidance, may our passion never cease,
May we never unwillingly put our Deity's flame
That burns within us all,
May nothing turn us away from the path
The Gods and Goddesses demand us tread,

May we always hold our heads up high
And know we are worthy of Deity's love.
Within us is strength, courage, conviction
If only we take the time to seek it.
May we always value the power of this circle
And do all in our power to keep it and all sacred places safe.
O Dread Southern Galla, steal away from thy lake of fire
And with us be joined as we humbly say hail and welcome.

West:
As I look to the West,
I call upon the Dreaded Galla of the West,
Guardian of the pools of black waters and the Western Gates.
Come fast, come strong.
Rain down upon us
With the strength of a thousand waterfalls.
Wash away the cobwebs from our eyes and heart.
Pour into our minds the dangers
Of always being as cold, hard, and rigid as ice,
Or always bending to the will of others
And trying to fit in by going with the crowd,
Taking the shape of one's surroundings as does water,
Or always threatening to go aloft to the astral realm
Or other planes of existence with fanatical spirituality
Or in the throes of our lust for knowledge and wisdom
Until becoming as discorporate as vapor.
Water is the teacher of the value of adaptaability,
Changing with the ebb and flow of the tides
While always remaining true to form.
So come, be with us,
Cleanse us from the excesses of our emotions
And the internal turmoil they can cause.
Open up our inner mystery,
Bathe our third eye with your magical waters
So we may see all worlds of darkness as well as light.

Brush our lips with but a drop of thy Queen's precious tears
So we may know Her by Her heart as well as face.
We seek out your realm not to drown but to swim,
Not to tread uninspiringly through stagnant ponds
But to glide effortlessly through all the streams of life.
Guide us to the way to our soul,
Guide us to true love's sweet embrace.
Even thy Queen stood not unmoved by its tender touch.
O dread Western Galla,
Steal away from thy waters dark and murky
So ours may be clear, and with us be joined
As we humbly say hail and welcome.

North:
As I look to the North,
I call upon the dread Galla of the north,
Guardian of Thy Queen's bounty,
All the treasures of the underworld and the Northern Gates.
Come fast, come strong,
Come with all the richness of thy realm
For indeed all that glitters is not gold
And deep within the dark soil of the earth
Can be found the greatest of treasures.
Bestow upon us thy grounding energy.
Help us keep our feet firmly planted on the ground.
Show us the true value of all within us
That society teaches us to hide or throw away
As trash into thy Queen's box of jewels.
Open our minds and hearts to what we hold most dear.
Teach us to guard them with all the ferocity that is yours.
Teach us the wisdom of thy Queen's sovereign rule.
To master is to nurture as well as teach and command,
To advise with a motherly touch as well as a father's strong hand.
Wherever we trek, may you be at our feet
Guiding us on the path to our infinite destiny.

Come forth, come forth from out of the bowels of the earth,
From out of the black pit of darkness into this circle's light.
We look to you to guide us to thy Queen's embrace.
May we all be as black pearls on Her most treasured strand
As to you O Northern Galla we say humbly hail and welcome.

Center:
As I stand in the center of this sacred space,
I call to the power and passion of the great God Nirgal,
Most beloved of His dark Queen.
Protect us on our journey to Her dark realm.
Let us not fear as we face Her tear-stained face,
Rather, as You did before us,
Let us tremble at Her great wisdom
And rejoice in Her ethereal beauty.
Like a gentle father, take us tenderly by the hand
And lead us in homage to Your Love's dark throne.
As Her deepest love and sole companion
In the dark abode that is Your home,
You lovingly opened Her wounded heart to passion
And the ecstasy of love's sweet embrace,
Open our hearts now to the searing touch of Your beloved Bride.
Let us not be blinded by Her power
But run to Her arms as an infant to its mother.
Guide us, Dark Lord on this path to wisdom
As to You we say hail and welcome.

Invocation to Ereshkigal:
Blessed Dark Mother Ereshkigal,
Mother of tears, Black Faced Queen of the Galla,
We invoke Thee and call Thee to be with us in this circle tonight.
You are not forgotten, You are not alone.
You possess more children than those of Your realm
Hidden deep within the bowels of the earth.
You have cried in the shadows for far too long.

Come, we beseech You, come dance in the light.

Come partake of our seeds of woe and sow

Your bitter field of broken dreams and shattered hearts.

You alone hallow the heart, Most Holy Mother of Sorrow.

Raise Your crop of misery.

Reap Your harvest of all our deepest and most primal fears.

We dare to taste of the fruit of Your infernal garden

And welcome Your lessons harsh though they be.

Come, O Queen, partake of our anger, bitterness,

Rage, envy, jealousy, hate,

All our cynicism and disenchantment of love's sweet touch,

Of the barreness of our hearts we hide from ourselves.

You rip to shreds with a gesture

What our sharpest blades would take a millenium to barely scratch.

You sear Your fiery essence deep within our souls.

You brand us with Your eyes, mark us with Your embrace.

No heart stands unmoved by Your barest whisper.

Come be with us, let us howl at the moon,

Shout at the wind, scream at the sky.

Too long have our spirits suffered in silence.

Help us exorcise the demons within that are yours to rule.

We are standing naked in the temple, vulnerable but unashamed,

Stripped of all our defenses but unafraid in Thy presence.

Come, O Ereshkigal, let us cry with Thee for awhile.

Despair have we all known.

May we be united in our sadness.

From You we seek not comfort or a mother's tender touch,

But all the wisdom that is Yours, however You choose to bestow it.

Hallow our hearts, Beloved Goddess.

To You Who guard the maelstrom from which we create our nightmares,

O Dreaded Queen, we say hail and welcome.

Anyone else who has a special invocation to Ereshkigal should also invoke Her at this time. When She is first invoked, Her presence hurts, especially the heart; however this soon eases and the sweetest, most precious knowledge may be bestowed.

Oracle of Ereshkigal:
My voice is heard in the howling of the damned.
Those who suffer invoke Me.
Bitterness is My throne, loneliness My salvation.
Bring Me these gifts and I will teach you survival.
I am the Black-faced Queen of the Galla.
I have been forgotten in your dark places,
The secret surfaces of your hearts that gleam like obsidian mirrors.
But I am there.
My jewels, My treasure-box are those things others discard.
I get the last, the least
So I learn to draw blood from shadow and I claim the bones.

Cry with Me.
Touch that darkest, barest place within your hearts.
I am loss that scalds the flesh.
I am envy and jealousy and hate, and I am all that lies beyond.
Madness is sometimes My gift:
They are like Me, the ones who have often seen too much.
I mend again the shattered heart.
I turn it to a field of glass.
My breath is the darkness that brings the cold chill of fear.
I have known love but it has not known Me.
I teach patient endurance.

I am the opener.
I take your pain, misery, barreness and loss
And with it weave My cloak.
I am the Barren One and I collect what others do not want,
All the things that make you see beyond the prisms of day's illusion.
I hallow the heart.

I am the One Who does not touch.
Seek Me where your loss is greatest.

I am beauty that scorns the light,
Lonely beauty and bitter rage.
I collect the fears you release.
You mistake Me and My place—darkness is not barren.
I am Mother to monsters, all your hidden fears
And I teach you to master yourselves. I lead you to light.

I am beyond death.
Pain is pleasure too for what it teaches.
Light without darkness is nothing at all.
I am the Goddess no one wants but all must seek.
I am the Mother of all loss.
I make sacred the spirit.
Fear is My greatest gift to you
For courage is a dark blade whose honing must be earned.
Bring Me offerings of wormwood for it is bitter like My heart.
I am the Eater of Corpses, flesh is My feast.
I am the ash that remains from the offering.
My gifts and My treasures are many to teach but I must be invited in.

At this point everyone should discuss the ways in which Ereshkigal has touched their lives. When this discussion is complete, Her box should be constructed.

Ereshkigal's Box:

A few weeks before the ritual is to take place, have all participants receive several of the below listed items (until all have been given out). The participants should meditate on how their items symbolize an aspect of Ereshkigal.

Cowrie shells
Dried pink rose buds
Dragon's blood incense
Black silk roses
Bones and/or skulls

Stones (obsidian, garnet, hematite, black crystal)

A dagger

A medusa image

A pomegranate and pomegranate seeds

Black feathers

Dark Moon Goddess oil

A pentacle

Cypress

An empty, elegant glass vial

A scrolled oracle of Ereshkigal (either the one in this rite, or one She chooses to bestow upon a devotee)

On the day of the ritual, have a space prepared in the center of the circle with a large wooden or wicker box with a black cloth covering the bottom, a bowel of graveyard dirt, a bowl of wormwood, a small clay Inanna figurine, three black cloths, a pestle, appropriate items for pricking the finger to draw blood (enough for each person to have their own). Everyone participating in the ritual should have an item of significant symbolic and/or sentimental value that they now wish to discard as well as the items they meditated upon. Finally, everyone should have prepared a short invocation honoring their forgotten ancestors whose names have been lost to antiquity, especially those that endured and triumphed over incredible hardships.

Preparing the Box

Smudge the box or basket inside and out with Ereshkigal's incense. All participants should be gathered in a circle and the incense should be continually burning during the preparation of the box. The smudge pot should be placed inside the box.

The graveyard dirt: This goes into the box first. Each participant should take the box and toss a handful of the dirt into the box while reciting their invocations (with deepest intent) to their ancestors as mentioned earlier. After the box has been completely passed around the circle, next comes....

The Inanna figure: This may also be done with each person bringing their own statue or picture. A few moments of silence while the circle prepares to intimately attune themselves to the power of the Goddess may prove beneficial before this next step. It is important to remember that Inanna descended to Ereshkigal's realm in search of wisdom. Ereshkigal fixed upon Her the eye of death and Inanna died. For three days and three nights Inanna's corpse hung in Ereshkigal's chamber then She was reborn whole within Herself. She had to face Ereshkigal and all the dark places within Herself before She could be called Queen of Heaven. For this next step, wrap the statue in one of the black cloths. Say, " I am Inanna and I willingly enter the realm of My sister Ereshkigal". Then smash the statue with the pestle. (If everyone is using their own picture, tear it, if everyone has their own statue, they should smash it when their turn comes.) Once everyone has had their turn, the wrapped remains are placed in the box.

It cannot be stressed enough that this act should only be done through Ereshkigal's will, in Her name and by Her hand. No feelings of sacrilege should invade this part of the ritual as the act is merely symbolic of the wrath Ereshkigal inflicted upon Inanna during the Great Descent. It is the smashing of all facades and barriers that keep us from Deity. During the smashing, the participant should openly and vocally strip himself or herself of all of his/her defenses as Inanna did before Ereshkigal, in perfect love and perfect trust.

Next the box itself is passed around the circle and each member in turn places the personal item they have chosen to discard inside. As they do so, each person should explain why they have selected this item and what significance, memories, scars it holds. Again, take as much time as necessary with this.

Wormwood: Have the circle prepare themselves for the intensity of the symbolism involved here. The box is passed around the circle with each participant tossing a handful of wormwood from the bowl into it then pricking his or her finger with an appropriate implement as mentioned before. Each person should have their own implement. Everyone should annoint some more wormwood with a few drops of their own blood and also toss this into the box. It should be focused in everyone's mind while performing this act that they are making a pact between themselves and

Ereshkigal and indeed all Deity. In this pact you are vowing that you and your group, circle, Iseum or coven will be the voice of all Deity, not just those that are easy to invoke. You are vowing to share any wisdom that They should choose to bestow. No Deity will be outcast, forgotten, or ignored because They are considered too dark, too violent, too uncontrollable in power, or worst of all, too malevolent. To not be open to the worship of all Deity is to not truly worship any Deity at all.

Pass the box and the bowel of wormwood around the circle as many times as possible. Each time it comes to them, the participant should take a pinch put it in the box and say the name of and oft-maligned or forgotten God or Goddess. Examples include: the Morrigan, Kali-ma, Hela, Sekhmet, Morbius, Hecate, Set, Yewe, Allat, Nebet-het (Nephthys), Anubis, Hades, Loki, etc. Then everyone participating should audibly state this pact with the utmost reverence and sincerity in their hearts while annointing the wormwood.

The items of meditation: The box should again be passed around the circle while each participant places in it one of the items they meditated on while explaining how that item represents or symbolizes Ereshkigal to them. This is done until all items except for the scrolled oracle and the glass vial. The vial should be filled with tears during the ritual if anyone is so moved otherwise it is to be filled with Ereshkigal 's incense.

Any insights or enlightenments received during the meditation should be shared and discussed. Then the filled vial and the scrolled oracle are added to the box. If a devotee's oracle has been used, it should be read aloud before it is added to the box. Another black cloth should be laid on top of everthing in the box then the box itself should be closed.

Thanksgiving:
Ereshkigal, Mother of longing
Whose quiet beauty illuminates the Kurnugia,
No longer do You go unremembered,
No longer must You sit forgotten in Your dark realm
While the praises of Your sister Inanna are sung.
Gladly we offer the darkest jewels of our deepest longing
To adorn Your gleaming diadem.

Our hearts are Yours, Queen of the Dark, Welcoming Earth.
No longer must You haunt the shadows,
No longer must You scrounge amongst garbage,
Taking only trash for Your treasure-box.
Here we bring You our own treasures,
Those things that have succored and guided us through our own trevail.
No longer are You given only that which is unwanted.
Tonight receive our gifts of love and homage.
Gladly will we visit you in Your dark hall,
Willingly shall we delight in the mystic rose of Your teaching.
You are always welcome in our temple and in our hearts.
Hail and farewell, Most Beloved Queen of Sorrow.

I will praise the Queen of Humankind,
I will praise Ereshkigal,
Queen of Humankind.
Among all the many Deities,
Ereshkigal is merciful.

(quoted from *Ancient Mirrors of Womanhood* by Merlin Stone)

Devocations:
As I stand in the center of this sacred temple,
Let my words echo back to the time of the beginning,
The time when Thy praises resounded in the halls of Sumer.
Great Lord Nirgal, take good care of Thy Beloved Queen.
Kindle the flame of joy in Her wounded heart, sweet Lord,
That Her song of passion may reach the vault of Heaven.
We praise Thee for Thy passion and valour.
We are Thy children, Lord, lead us gently by the hand
As we seek the arms of Thy bride.
Let the flame of Thy virile spirit illuminate the path before us.
We thank You for watching over our descent this night,
Guide us always with Thy wisdom as we say hail and farewell.

North:

O Galla of the North, thy Mother cries out.

Her breasts hunger for the caress of Her suckling child.

Make haste to Her nurturing bosom She offers to so few,

As to you we give thanks for showing us the fullness of our bounty

And how even our pain and our grief can be a kind of treasure.

We give unto you all our excess energy.

Take it to thy Queen as our offering unto Her.

Ground us with thy touch, nurture us with thy embrace.

Tell us with thy voice the way in which we should go.

Help us not to fear when we shall walk the halls you roam

For we are children of many mothers

Watching over all our births and deaths.

Teach us to be patient for all within us

For to manifest for a flood saves not a countryside in drought.

Thy Queen's name we hold close to our hearts.

Here in this place She has found a temple.

Within us is a jewel burning bright with Her flame,

Cold and stark but no lesser in brilliance than our own mighty sun.

Be off, go now ever quickly back to Thy abyss

Knowing here are those who need and love you.

O Northern Galla, hail and farewell.

West:

O Kurgarra of the West, thy Queen awaits.

The Black Lakes of Her realm are in need of thy attendance.

Make haste to Her side as to thee we give thanks for thy wisdom

You have poured down upon us from thy vessels of knowledge.

May we keep your teachings close to our hearts

And weave all our emotions into a glorious web,

Delicate in finery and beauty but unbreakable in strength.

May our third eye always discern all that may come our way

And may we interpret accurately

All images and feelings our gifts may supply.

We leave you with our gifts of tears and laughter,

Of love and hate forever intertwined within us all.

May you always be there teaching us how to survive in your waters

And never succumb to any flood or whirlpool we meet in life.

Guide us to love. Guide us to glory.

Open our hearts to the essence of thy Queen.

She calls, She calls, She is summoning you back.

Be off to thy realm knowing here you are always welcome

As on your parting from our circle, we say hail and farewell.

South:

O Kurgarra of the South, do you not hear the calling of thy name?

Thy Queen needs Her guardians of the sacred hellfire.

Burn a path to Her feet as to thee we give thanks

For bestowing upon us the strength of will

To not cower but stand steadfast

And learn from all the Deities may show us.

May we never forget the preciousness

Of our flames of passion and knowledge of self.

May we never fear the power that lies within us all.

May we always find courage and confidence

Within ourselves through all situations

And when things become too great may we always remember

Thy Queen's and all Deities' blessed sacred names.

We have been baptised by your fire

And are touched by thy kindness of granting to us

Your gift of what you guard so well.

And guard you must, so be off in haste,

Knowing here you shall always have a home

And in your and thy Queen's honor

We shall always keep our flames burning proud and strong

As to you we say hail and farewell.

East:

O Kurgarra of the East, thy Queen draws you near.

Her blade is in need of sharpening upon the stone.

Be off to Her bidding as to you we give thanks
For showing us the power of our breath and words and song
And from tearing us away from the selves we think we are.
By your grace and kindness, can we soar unencumbered
Swift and free like a mighty hawk in flight,
All hopelessness and despair our prey.
May you always guard our hearts and our tongues
And teach us to breathe life into all we do.
The gift of incense we bestow unto you with all our love.
May we always revere the darkness as well as the light.
May we never fear thy Queen's blade that cuts away all not of us.
All that is anathema to Deity's touch.
May we never fear Her face that reflects all that we are
With all the coldness of an obsidian mirror.
She is calling, She is summoning with Her voice.
Your aid is required for Her will to be done.
Be off to they abyss knowing here you can breathe freely always
As to you we say hail and farewell.

Closing Chant:

Inanna is ascending, She is rising, She is rising. Come, let us go to Inanna!

Sources: *Ancient Mirrors of Womanhood,* Stone, Merlin. Beacon Press, 1979. *Myths from Mesopotamia,* Dalley, Stephanie (trans.). Oxford University Press, 1989. *Inanna: Queen of Heaven and Earth,* Wolkstein, Diane. Harper and Row, 1983. *The Women's Encyclopedia of Myths and Secrets,* Walker, Barbara. Harper San Francisco, 1983. *In the Wake of the Goddess,* Frymer-Kensky, Tikva. Fawcett Columbine, 1992.

I am indebted to our High Priest Hierophant Jason Barnes for his wisdom and assistance in working with Ereshkigal.

First published in The Beltane Papers *Issue #27 Spring 2001*

Ritual for the Day of Inanna

First published in Pagan Book of Hours *by First Kingdom Church of Asphodel, (2006). MA: Asphodel Press. Used with permission.*

Invocation to Inanna

I say, "Hail!" to the Holy One who appears in the heavens!
I say, "Hail!" to the Holy Priestess of Heaven!
I say, "Hail!" to Inanna, Great Lady of Heaven!
Holy Torch! You fill the sky with light!
You brighten the day at dawn!
I say, "Hail!" to Inanna, Great Lady of Heaven!
Awesome Lady of the Annuna Gods!
Crowned with great horns,
You fill the heavens and earth with light!
At evening the radiant star, the great light fills the sky,
The Lady of the Evening comes bravely forth from heaven,
The people in all the lands lift their eyes to Her,
The ox in his yoke lows for her,
The sheep stir up the dust in their fold,
The beasts, the many living creatures of the steppe,
The lush gardens and orchards, the green reeds and trees,
The fish of the Deep and the birds of Heaven,
Inanna makes them hurry to their sleeping places.
I say, "Hail!" to Inanna, First Daughter of the Moon!
Mighty, majestic, and radiant,
You shine brilliantly in the evening,
You brighten the day at dawn,
You stand in the heavens like the sun and the moon,
Your wonders are known both above and below,
To the greatness of the Holy Priestess of Heaven,
To you, Inanna, I sing!

Upon a cloth of white and silver place tablets of soft clay, a stylus, a box with the sigil of Inanna, a clay rosette, the Knot of Inanna, and many silver stars. After the ritual, approach the altar and write a single word with the stylus in each tablet of soft clay, and place it in the box. The next year, take out and display the dried tablets of the previous years, and add more. After the invocation is read, each goes forward to add their word to the clay tablets. These can be used as divination later, in succeeding years.

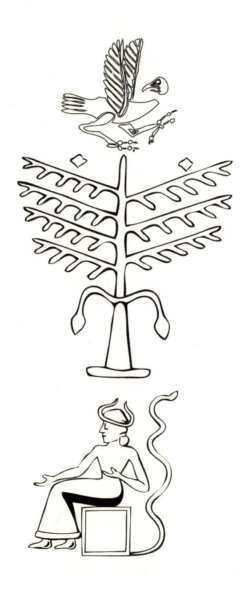

The Sharing of the *Me*—A Ritual to the Goddess Inanna
Galina Krasskova

This ritual was originally performed by Iseum of the Star*Eyed Warrior c. 1998. "Me" is a Sumerian word for specific powers, skills, and blessings bestowed upon the Goddess Inanna by Her father.

Before the ritual, the priest/ess should take a stack of small index cards. On each card, she should write one of the *me*. These cards should then be shuffled and placed on the altar, which should also include images and symbols sacred to the Goddess Inanna. The *me* include:

- Love Given and Received
- Self-Awareness
- Self-Reliance
- Success
- The Craft of the Scribe
- Laughter
- The Art of Lamentation
- The Art of Counseling
- The Art of Physical Healing
- The Gift of Prophecy
- Strength
- Pain
- The Art of Teaching
- Truth
- The Art of the Ordeal
- The Gift of Marriage
- The Art of Cruelty
- The Art of Gift-Giving
- The Art of Lovemaking
- Disappointment
- Patience
- Temperance
- The Art of Nurturing
- Power
- The Art of Mental Health
- The Crown of Priesthood
- The Art of Treachery
- The Gift of a Secure Dwelling Place
- The Art of Reaching Goals
- The Art of Planning
- The Gift of the Ascent
- Anger and Rage
- Joy
- The Gift of Song
- Intelligence
- Courage
- The Art of Discipline
- The Gift of Friendship
- Integrity
- Fulfillment
- The Art of Kindness
- The Art of Survival
- The Art of Forgiveness
- The Art of Play
- The Art of Time Management

- The Art of Effective Speech
- Dismay
- The Gift of Empathy
- Pleasure
- The Art of Decision-Making
- The Gift of Music
- The Art of Efficiency
- Beauty
- Endurance
- The Gift of Mediumship
- Common Sense
- Intuition
- The Art of Learning
- Culinary Artistry
- The Art of Dance
- A Sense of Purpose
- The Craft of the Bard
- The Craft of the Artist
- The Art of Listening
- The Gift of Communing with the Gods
- The Art of Compassion

- The Sword
- The Art of Judging
- Passion
- The Crown of Kingship
- Fear
- Faith
- Tranquility
- The Gift of the Descent
- The Art of Magic
- Solitude
- The Craft of the Warrior
- The Art of Parenting
- Humility
- Respect
- The Art of Leadership
- The Art of Spiritual Healing
- The Gift of Sight
- The Art of Design
- Poetry
- The Gift of Devotion
- Love
- The Art of Ritual

The priest/ess should meditate and pray to Inanna as s/he is writing these out. If, through this time of discernment, s/he feels that Inanna wishes more qualities to be added to the list of *me* then the priest/ess should include them.

An altar to Inanna should be set up. It should have an image of Inanna if possible. There should be flowers, candles, incense, and an offering bowl in front of the image. The priest/ess should consecrate the space in whatever manner is customary for him/her. The candles and incense should be lit.

Invocation to Inanna

Hail to Inanna, Queen of Heaven.

Hail to Inanna, Bright Star of Evening.

Hail to Inanna, Holy Priestess of the Gods.

Hail to Inanna, Keeper of the *Me*.

Hail to Inanna, Beautiful and proud.

Hail to Inanna, Ornament of the Heavens.

Hail to Inanna, Supreme in Her Power.

Hail to Inanna, Who made the Descent.

Hail to Inanna, Who swallowed Her fear.

Hail to Inanna, Who nurtured Her courage.

Hail to Inanna, Who sacrificed Her pride.

Hail to Inanna, Who embraced humility.

Hail to Inanna, Who laid down Her power.

Hail to Inanna, Who learned the Art of Supplication.

Hail to Inanna, Who journeyed to the Great Below.

Hail to Inanna, Prostrate before Her Sister.

Hail to Inanna, Who sought wisdom on the meat hook.

Hail to Inanna, Who sang Ereshkigal's praises.

Hail to Inanna, Who sacrificed for Her knowledge.

Hail to Inanna, Redeemed by sacrifice.

Hail to Inanna, Bestower of blessings.

We will praise the Queen of Heaven.

We will praise the First Daughter of the Moon.

We will praise the Holy One of the Huluppu throne.

We will praise Inanna.

Praise Her.

Praise Her.

We praise Inanna.

(The priest/ess should pour out an offering of good wine into the offering bowl.)

Each person takes a turn hailing Inanna as a chalice of wine or sweet juice is passed around the circle. The priest/ess reads, chants, or retells the story of Inanna receiving the *me* from Her father. The book *Inanna: Queen of Heaven and Earth* by Diane Wolkstein and Samuel Kramer has a beautiful translation of the relevant texts.

Prayer to Inanna:

"Holy Inanna, Keeper of the *me,* Bestower of Blessings, Wise Queen, Mightly Goddess smile upon us tonight, we who are gathered in Your honor. Grant us understanding and the gift of discernment as we seek to explore the blessings that have been given to us to hold. Through the sharing of *me,* may we draw closer to You, and come to comprehend, perhaps just a little bit more, the path we are meant to walk. Hail Inanna, Great Queen of Heaven and earth. Hear us, Great Lady, this night. Please hear our prayer."

The priest/ess takes the index cards from the altar, explaining that upon each card, s/he has written the name of one of the *me.* Throughout our lives and spiritual journeys, we receive a measure of blessings. Sometimes those blessings a are very obviously blessings and sometimes they occur in the form of challenges. As we grow and progress in our spiritual lives, sometimes we must consciously sacrifice certain blessings to gain others. Sometimes we must leap blindly into the abyss, trusting that the Gods will hold us up. While there are many *me,* more than would be possible to count and list in any ritual, no one, no matter how favored by the Gods he or she may be, receives them all. Sometimes we may not even realize what blessings have been poured into us. That too, is a process of discovery blessed by the Goddess Inanna.

The cards should be shuffled again. Each person in the circle is dealt seven cards, one for each gate Inanna passed through on Her descent into the Underworld of Ereshkigal. After giving people a few moments to examine and think about their *me,* the priest/ess should inform them, that they may choose to keep, discard, or give two of their cards away to the others. If a card is discarded, another may be chosen from the deck. Each person should end up with at least seven cards by the end of this transaction.

Next, each person should lay the one deemed most precious to him/her, face down to the side. People should then share and discuss three that have been kept in the hand. Finally, share the most important card, the one put to the side earlier. Share why it is important, what it means to you. Now comes the homework:

- ❖ For the next seven days, carry it with you. Meditate on it.
- ❖ Each night, light a candle and offer a prayer to Inanna.
- ❖ After praying to Inanna, work on creating a representation of this *me*, this thing you hold most precious. It could be a collage, a reliquary box filled with items representative of this thing, a collection of poetry, anything that speaks of this particular *me*.
- ❖ At the end of seven nights, hold a personal ritual to Inanna and burn your creation. Sacrifice it to Inanna just as She sacrificed Her *me* at the seven gates to Ereshkigal's realm.

Those gathered should share food and drink, as they discuss any insights discovered during the sharing out of the *me*.

Closing Prayer
We praise Inanna,
Queen of Heaven.
We praise Inanna,
Gracious Counselor.
We praise Inanna,
Now and forever.

Psychopomp's Prayer Ritual
Raven Kaldera
Originally published in Hermaphrodeities, *Asphodel Press 2010.*
Used with permission

There are a lot of rituals out there in the world for someone who is going through an underworld period ... and yet there still aren't enough, because such rituals are usually so personal that they must be created personally for each person. On the other hand, I've never seen anything for the loved one who is going through their own problems but whom you cannot directly help. In cases like that, asking for greater help is often necessary. This ritual is specifically for third gender people who are going through a period of depression, sorrow, or bad times, but it can be used for anyone who is in the middle of Inanna's descent and who you cannot directly help.

You will need four black candles for this rite, placed at the four directions around you so that you must turn to light them one at a time.

(Light the candle in the North, and say:)
O Guardians of the Gateway to the Darkness,
One who is in my thoughts has taken your road
And passed into the realm of dust and shadow.
Kurgarra, galatur,
Sister-brother, brother-sister,
Sprung from Earth, be solid as Earth,
Walk with them through the dark gates,
Let their feet never stumble,
Give them guidance when they fall from the path
And light one spark to see the road ahead.

(Light the candle in the West, and say:)
Gods of the Darkness, hold this one gently
And let their trials and troubles be only
What they need, and no more, and let them survive.
Kurgarra, galatur,

Sister-brother, brother-sister,
Sprung from Earth, be solid as Earth,
Weep for them at the dark throne as I weep,
Show all the Gods below that they are cared for
And deserve release once they have done their work.
(If one can shed tears for them, this would be a good thing.)

(Light the candle in the South, and say:)
Gods of the Darkness, pass this one through your fires
And keep them hung like a corpse
Only for a short time; let the sacred hands
On which I call take them down and lay them out.
Kurgarra, galatur,
Sister-brother, brother-sister,
Sprung from Earth, be solid as Earth,
Let the food of life pass their lips!
Let the water of life pass their lips!
Let them be made whole again.

(Light the candle in the East, and say:)
Guardians of the Gateway to the Darkness,
Release this one in good time,
Keep them no longer than is necessary.
Kurgarra, galatur,
Sister-brother, brother-sister,
Sprung from Earth, be solid as Earth,
Walk with them through the opening gates,
Let their feet never stumble,
And may each portal split asunder
And bring them once again into the light.
(Let each candle burn down until it goes out.)

The next ritual incorporates the Art of the Ordeal. Ordeal work often involves the careful application of pain to create an altered state of consciousness, or to achieve another spiritual goal, such as greater receptivity to one's Gods, or the making of an offering. Ordeal work can be one of the many paths to achieving an altered state (See "Dark Moon Rising" by R. Kaldera). Other practices, designed to induce trance and create a state of spiritual receptivity include prayer and meditation, ritual work, the use of rhythm and dance, ascetic practices such as fasting, the use of enthneogenic plants, sacred sex or sexually based practices, and divine possession. These practices have been used throughout history and across religions. It is not about pain, though that is a common tool used in these practices, but about rendering one utterly open to one's Gods.

The Descent Of Inanna

Raven Kaldera
Originally published in Dark Moon Rising, *Asphodel Press 2010.*
Used With Permission

The Descent of Inanna ritual is based on the original ancient texts from the Enuma Elish and other similar texts. The original story contained graphic violence, including sexual violence, and this ritual is a mystery play that includes those elements in a stylized, choreographed way. The amount of sexual contact and violence should be worked out ahead of time—and probably privately rehearsed—between the participants. I strongly suggest that anyone who is cast as Ereshkigal or the Annunaki/Galla have training in inflicting such activities in a safe way.

It is meant to be read by two narrators, one of whom reads the original lines, printed in bold type, and one who reads the modern commentary, printed in normal type. The characters mime the action described and the sections that are written in italics. The parts should be chosen wisely, especially that of Inanna; to star in this ritual is to call the myth of Inanna into your life. The part of Inanna should be played by someone who is willing to honor the descent into the darkness, and understands what it entails.

Performance notes: The individuals who play the parts of Inanna, Dumuzi, and Geshtinanna should have a certain amount of say in who plays the Annunaki and Ereshkigal. They should be reasonably comfortable with sexual contact and choreographed violence by each of them, and should ideally work out beforehand with these people what will be done to them, even if only for two minutes. The dialog is written to be spoken by the narrators, but could also be spoken by the players if they are able to memorize and recite lines under stress. Key dialogue can be given to the players, for added effect. Good choices are the lines at each of the gates ("What is this?" "Quiet, Inanna, the ways of the Underworld are perfect; they may not be questioned"), Dumuzi's "You! What are you doing here?", and the demons' "He can never escape us." Repeated lines ("Yet it must be done.", "Hunt him! Hunt Him!", "His doom is upon him.") can be spoken in unison by those watching.

All penetration (mimed or otherwise) is written to be done with strap-on dildoes, but it can be done with live genitalia if the individuals in question are comfortable with that. While we chose the activities that we thought would be the most appropriate for each gate, this too can be altered and redesigned by participants. The first time that we did this ritual, the last three Annunaki were all lovers of the woman who played Inanna, and so the genital contact did actually occur.

The Characters

Two Narrators

Inanna, the Queen of Heaven: Female. Should have a strong, proud presence but will willing to be stripped, humiliated, tormented, and beaten. Keep in mind that the character of Inanna is not submissive, but a powerful, dominant woman who chooses to submit in order to gain wisdom. The Inanna participant must be someone who is willing and able to endure periods of pain that she has no power to stop or control. This ritual should not be interrupted except for extreme, injurious accidental emergencies, so it is essential to thoroughly discuss what level of intensity is appropriate. Inanna should start with a blue gown covered in stars, which she shucks at the beginning of the play in order to don her "power" garb.

Ereshkigal, the Queen of the Underworld: Dominant female. Should also have great presence, and be able to wield some kind of beating implement. She should wear black robes/clothing, revealing or not, as works for the situation.

Ninshubur, Inanna's maidservant: A warrior woman, very devoted to Inanna. This is a good part for a service-oriented woman who is nonetheless an independent and strong person, and who puts that strength squarely in the service of another, or would like to. Ninshubur is personal assistant, bodyservant, and bodyguard. Ninshubur should wear red or orange, as befits a warrior; she should have short hair or wear a head-wrap, and carry a knife at her belt.

Dumuzi, Inanna's husband: Male. He is beaten and tormented for at least five to ten minutes during the course of the ritual, and should be able to deal with that.

Geshtinanna, Dumuzi's sister: Female. She is beaten and tormented for at least five to ten minutes during the course of the ritual, and should be able to endure this.

The Annunaki/The Galla: Seven tormentors, of varying genders. These seven people will play first the Annunaki, the judges and gate-guardians of the Underworld who torment and humiliate Inanna, and then the Galla, demons who follow Inanna up from the Underworld and torture Dumuzi and Geshtinanna. Should be competent at their job, and should be trusted by the three people that they will have to torment for a few minutes each. One of them should be Neti, the keeper of the first gate, referred to as male in the texts, and he will have an extra miming part.

Enlil, the Sun God: Miming part, no sexual contact. Wears a sun mask.

Nanna, the Moon God: Miming part, no sexual contact. Wears a moon mask.

Enki, the Inventor God: Miming part, no sexual contact. but a good deal of acting.

The Kurgarra and Galatur: Two transgendered individuals, one male-to-female and one female-to-male. Miming part only.

The Ritual

Drumbeats. Inanna sits on her throne, on the opposite side of the area from where Ereshkigal's throne lies behind a dark-colored curtain. As the first lines are read, she stands as if listening to something, and then wanders back and forth looking more and more dissatisfied. She slowly comes down into the front area, where a table is set up with her ritual garb on it.

From the Great Above
She opened her ear to the Great Below.
Inanna, the Queen of Heaven, had everything.
From the Great Above
The goddess opened her ear to the Great Below.

She was powerful. She was beautiful.
She ruled over love, war, and fertility.

From the Great Above
Inanna opened her ear to the Great Below.

All men and women bowed before her...
And yet something was missing from her life.

The Lady abandoned heaven and earth
To descend to the underworld.

All was light in her life. There was no darkness...
And no depth.

Inanna abandoned heaven and earth
To descend to the underworld.

Inanna heard the call of the dark places.

In Uruk she abandoned her temple
To descend to the underworld.

For the dark called her, seductively, compellingly.

In Badtibira she abandoned her temple
To descend to the underworld.

For the dark called her like the voice of a lover.

In Zabalam she abandoned her temple
To descend to the underworld.

For the dark called her in a terrifying voice.

In Adab she abandoned her temple
To descend to the underworld.

For the dark whispered to her in her dreams.

In Nippur she abandoned her temple
To descend to the underworld.

For the dark touched her
With hands as light as a ghost.

In Kish she abandoned her temple
To descend to the underworld.

For the dark sang to her in the wind through her hair.

In Akkad she abandoned her temple
To descend to the underworld.

For the Call of the Darkness will not be denied.

To the Land of No Return she was determined to go.

For when the Darkness calls, finally, you come.

To the dark house, dwelling of Irkalla's goddess,

You go down to the dark place, one way or another.

To the house which those who enter cannot leave,

Perhaps you go unwillingly,

Like a rape, like a violation.

On the road where traveling is one-way only,

Perhaps you go with screams and weeping.

To the house where those who enter are deprived of light,

Would it not be better to go willingly,

As if to your wedding day?

Where dust is their food, clay their bread.

Who lives in the darkness that you fear?

They see no light, they dwell in darkness,

Yet the dark does not stop their vision.

They are clothed like birds, with feathers.

For they have lightened themselves

Of the pain they carry.

Over the door and the bolt, dust has settled.

For few are brave enough to take this path.

Inanna stands before the table, and removes her garment. She is naked beneath it, with her back to the audience. As the next lines are read, she methodically dresses herself in the following garments: a silver crown with a large many-pointed star on it, a long strand of blue beads that goes around her neck twice, a lightweight cloak of blue studded with stars that ties around her neck, a belt of links set with stones, eye makeup—have her already made up and just mime putting a little more on—and a metallic gold strapless bra or corset, and a large gold bracelet. A blue rod, like a sceptre, should be there for her to pick up and take with her. As soon as she walks away, the table is removed.

She gathered together the seven me.
She gathered together
All the worldly powers she had won.
She took them into her hands.
With the me in her possession, she prepared herself:
She placed the shugurra,
The crown of the steppe, on her head.
For she would go down to the Underworld
As the queen that she was.
She arranged the locks of hair across her forehead.
For she would have none see her as less than perfect.
She tied the lapis beads around her neck.
Let the double strand of beads fall to her breast,
For all the wealth of Heaven was hers.
And wrapped the royal robe around her body.
For she held the mysteries of womanhood within her.
She hung the girdle of birthstones about her hips.
For she was proud to be the Jewel of the Sky.
She daubed her eyes with the ointment called
'Let him come, let him come.'
For her beauty had gained her entrance
To many a narrow place.
Bound the breast plate called 'Come, man, come!'
Around her chest,
For she was justly proud of the loveliness of her body.
Slipped the gold ring over her wrist,
For she would be reminded of her husband
And her marriage.
And took the lapis measuring rod and line in her hand.
For she was used to measuring and judging
All she saw.
And Inanna set out for the underworld.

Inanna walks toward the first Gate of the Underworld, which can be an archway, or just a space where Neti, the Gatekeeper, stands. During the next lines, she takes Ninshubur by the shoulders and mimes speaking to her earnestly.

Ninshubur, her faithful servant, went with her.

Inanna spoke to her, saying:

'Ninshubur, my constant support,

My sukkal who gives me wise advice,

My warrior who fights by my side,

I am descending to the Kur, to the underworld.

If I do not return,

Set up a lament for me by the ruins.

If I do not return in three days, get help.

Get help any way that you can.

Beat the drum for me in the assembly places.

Circle the houses of the gods.

Do not let them forget me.

Tear at your eyes, at your mouth, at your thighs.

Dress yourself in a single garment like a beggar.

My life may depend on your aid.

Go to Nippur, to the temple of Enlil.

When you enter his holy shrine, cry out:

"Oh, Father Enlil, do not let your daughter

Be put to death in the underworld."

If Enlil will not help you,

Go to Ur, to the temple of Nanna.

Weep before Father Nanna.

If Nanna will not help you,

Go to Eridu, to the temple of Enki.

Weep before Father Enki.

Father Enki, the God Of Wisdom, knows the food of life,

He knows the water of life;

Knows the secret of life.

Surely he will not let me die.'

Inanna turns and walks toward the First Gate. Ninshubur stands straight, but is clearly afraid for her. The following lines are said with decreasing volume and certainty.

Surely someone can save me.
Surely someone can save me.
Surely someone can save me.
Inanna continued on her way to the underworld.

Inanna stops and looks back one more time, and gestures to Ninshubur.

Then she stopped and said: 'Go now Ninshubur—
Do not forget the words I have commanded you.'
For my life rests on the turn of a blade
For my life rests on the touch of a feather
For my life is no longer my own.

Inanna approaches the First Gate, and mimes knocking. Drumbeats sound for her knocks. She gestures with her arms as she makes the threats to Neti.

When Inanna arrived at the outer gates of the underworld,
She knocked loudly.
For who among us can resist a show of courage
At the door of Death?
She cried out in a fierce voice: "Open the door, gatekeeper!
Open the door, Neti! I alone would enter!
If you do not open the gate for me to come in,
I shall smash the door and shatter the bolt,
I shall smash the doorpost and overturn the doors,
I shall raise up the dead and they shall eat the living:
The dead shall outnumber the living!"
The Dead already outnumber the living, Inanna,
And they cannot be moved by your words.

Neti stands forward with his spear and thumps it into the ground, looking forbidding. He and Inanna gesture at each other during this conversation.

Neti, the chief gatekeeper of the kur, asked: "Who are you?"
She answered: "I am Inanna, Queen of Heaven,
On my way to the East."
Neti said: "If you are truly Inanna, Queen of Heaven,
On your way to the East,
Why has your heart led you on the road
From which no traveler returns?"
If you are the Queen of Heaven,
Then you are truly in the wrong place.
Why are you really here?

Inanna turns her head as if in thought, and wraps her mantle closer about her. For the first time, she seems unsure of herself.

Inanna answered: "Because... of my older sister Ereshkigal,
Her husband, Gugalanna, the Bull of Heaven, has died.
I have come to witness the funeral rites.
Let the beer of his funeral rites be poured into the cup.
Let it be done."

Inanna bows her head.

I have come to witness a funeral,
Although I fear it will be my own.
Let it be done.
Let it be done.
Let it be done.
Neti spoke: "Stay here Inanna, I will speak to my queen.
I will give her your message."
I will tell her of your pride,
And of your hubris.

Neti turns and goes toward the curtain, which opens. Ereshkigal is seated on her throne. He kneels before her; she touches the head of her loyal servant.

Neti, the chief gatekeeper of the Kur,
Entered the palace of Ereshkigal, the Queen of the Underworld, and said:
"My Queen, a maiden
As tall as heaven, as wide as the earth,
As strong as the foundations of the city wall,
Waits outside the palace gates.
The smell of Life is upon her
Like a summer breeze over the warm fields.
She has gathered together the seven me.
She has taken them in her hands.
With the me in her possession, she has prepared herself:
She wears her power like a glimmering mantle.
On her head she wears the shurgarra,
The crown of the steppe.
She speaks as if she is used to being obeyed.
Across her forehead her dark locks of hair
Are carefully arranged.
She looks as if many hands toiled for her loveliness.
Around her neck she wears the double strand of lapis beads.
She glitters with the wealth of the Land Above.
Around her hips hangs the girdle of birthstones.
She glitters with the stars of the night sky.
Her body is wrapped in the royal robe.
All who look upon her know that she is a queen.
Her eyes are daubed with the ointment
'Let him come, let him come.'
She carries herself as if she knows her own beauty.
Around her chest she wears the breast plate called
'Come, man, come!'
She carries herself as if her beauty
Is her greatest power.

On her wrist she wears the gold ring.
You can be sure that she does not sleep alone.
In her hand she carries the lapis measuring rod and line."
She looks upon our dusty gate
And judges us with her eyes.

During the next lines, Ereshkigal mimes her anger, from resentment to outright rage. She stands up and stalks back and forth across the area, slapping various things with her sceptre, which can be a riding crop or something like it. She shakes her fist and gestures to the words.

When Erishkigal heard this,
She slapped her thigh and bit her lip.
She took the matter into her heart and dwelt on it.
Inanna appeared like a vision of all that she was not.
Her face grew livid as cut tamarisk,
She has beauty and grace.
Her lips grew dark as the rim of a kuninu-vessel.
She has the morning and evening sky.
"What brings her to me? What has incited her against me?
She has the wealth of the storehouse.
Surely not because I drink water with the Anunnaki,
She wears a golden crown on her head.
I eat clay for bread, I drink river-mud for beer!
She has the love and reverence of all people.
I have to weep for young men
Forced to abandon their sweethearts.
She has a living husband.
I have to weep for girls wrenched from their lover's laps.
No one weeps when Death weeps.
For the infant child I have to weep, expelled before its time."
If she wants the Great Below, I will give it to her.

Ereshkigal turns and points imperiously at Neti.

Then she spoke: "Come, Neti,
My chief gatekeeper of the Kur,
Heed my words:
Bolt the seven gates of the underworld.
Then, one by one, open each gate a crack.
Let Inanna enter.
As she enters, remove her royal garments.
Let the holy priestess of heaven enter bowed low."
Let her learn what secrets the darkness truly holds.
Neti heeded the words of his queen.

Neti turns and goes back to the gate, where Inanna has stood motionless.

He bolted the seven gates of the underworld.

The six other Annunaki come forth and stand beyond Neti, each a good distance away from each other. One at a time, they hold out staffs or wands horizontally as if to bar the way, in time to loud single drumbeats, symbolizing the locking of the gates.

Then he opened the outer gate.
He said to the maiden: "Come, Inanna, enter."

Neti puts his spear aside and bows, gesturing her to come through. She starts forward.

When she entered the first gate,
From her head, the shugurra, the crown of the steppe,
Was removed.

Neti reaches out and snatches the crown from her head. He tosses it to the side.

Inanna asked: "What is this?"
She was told: "Quiet, Inanna,

The ways of the underworld are perfect.
They may not be questioned."

Neti seizes her by her hair and slams her up against the gate, slaps her on the "Quiet, Inanna" line, and does some terribly painful thing to her for about two minutes.

For your power in the upper world
Means nothing here.
Your crown is dust and your legions are nothing.
And without them, who are you?

The second Annunaki steps forward next to the gate. Neti goes to stand beside Ereshkigal's throne. Inanna attempts to enter the gate again. The second Annunaki grabs her by the necklace and yanks it off her throat. Then the second Annunaki takes her by the throat, slaps her on the "Quiet, Inanna" line, and does something painful to her for about two minutes.

When she entered the second gate,
From her neck the double strand of lapis beads
Were removed.
Inanna asked: "What is this?"
She was told: "Quiet, Inanna,
The ways of the underworld are perfect.
They may not be questioned."
For your precious possessions mean nothing here.
The things you love to touch are dust
And your hands are empty.
And without them, who are you?

The third Annunaki steps forward next to the gate. The second Annunaki goes to stand beside Ereshkigal's throne. Inanna passes through the gate a third time. The third Annunaki tears the girdle from her hips, strikes her on the "Quiet, Inanna" line, and beats her ass for about two minutes.

When she entered the third gate,
From her hips the girdle of birthstones was removed.
Inanna asked: "What is this?"
She was told: "Quiet, Inanna,
The ways of the underworld are perfect,
They may not be questioned."
For your wealth means nothing here.
Your money is dust and you cannot buy your way out.
And without that, who are you?

The fourth Annunaki steps forward next to the gate. The third Annunaki goes to stand beside Ereshkigal's throne. Inanna passes through the gate a fourth time. The fourth Annunaki removes the bra/corset from her torso, strikes her on the "Quiet, Inanna" line, and does something painful to her breasts for about two minutes.

When she entered the fourth gate,
From her chest the breast plate called "Come, man, come!" was removed.
Inanna asked: "What is this?"
She was told, "Quiet, Inanna,
The ways of the underworld are perfect.
They may not be questioned."
For your beauty means nothing here.
Your sexual power is useless
and no one will look on you with desire.
And without that, who are you?

The fifth Annunaki steps forward next to the gate. The fourth Annunaki goes to stand beside Ereshkigal's throne. Inanna passes through the gate a fifth time. The fifth Annunaki takes the bracelet from her wrist, strikes her on the "Quiet, Inanna" line, buckles cuffs onto her wrists, and does something painful to her for about two minutes.

When she entered the fifth gate,
From her wrist the gold ring was removed.
Inanna asked: "What is this?"
She was told: "Quiet, Inanna,
The ways of the underworld are perfect.
They may not be questioned."
For your relationships with others mean nothing here.
You are alone
Without any other soul to come at your call.
And without them, who are you?

The sixth Annunaki steps forward next to the gate. The fifth Annunaki goes to stand beside Ereshkigal's throne. Inanna passes through the gate a sixth time, clearly stumbling, still clutching the rod. The sixth Annunaki takes it away from her, strikes her on the "Quiet, Inanna" line, and does something painful to her for about two minutes, probably with the rod, ideally breaking it in two in the process.

When she entered the sixth gate,
From her hand the lapis measuring rod and line was removed.
Inanna asked: "What is this?"
She was told: "Quiet, Inanna,
The ways of the underworld are perfect.
They may not be questioned."
For your mind and your intellect mean nothing here.
The ways in which you judge things,
Your values and your scales,
They are all useless in this place,
And without them, who are you?

The seventh Annunaki steps forward next to the gate. The sixth Annunaki goes to stand beside Ereshkigal's throne. Inanna crawls through the gate and is seized by the seventh Annunaki, who rips off her mantle, leaving her naked, strikes her on the "Quiet, Inanna" line, and then throws her down and roughly penetrates her (or mimes penetrating her) with a large strap-on dildo.

When she entered the seventh gate,
From her body the royal robe was removed.
Inanna asked: "What is this?"
She was told: "Quiet, Inanna,
The ways of the underworld are perfect.
They may not be questioned."
For your womanhood means nothing here.
The rules you live by are dust,
The role you lived is nothing,
For gender and roles mean nothing to the Dead.
And without that, who are you?

The seventh Annunaki drags her by her hair before the throne of Ereshkigal. The others converge on her, and she is strung up facing the audience. All seven strike her to pass judgment.

Naked and bowed low, Inanna entered the throne room.
Ereshkigal rose from her throne.
Inanna started toward the throne.
The Annunaki, the judges of the underworld,
Surrounded her.
They passed judgment against her.

Ereshkigal steps down from her throne. She takes up an implement and beats Inanna for about two minutes. Inanna sinks down in her bonds as if beaten down in spirit.

Then Erishkigal fastened on Inanna the eye of death.
She spoke against her the word of wrath.
She uttered against her the cry of guilt.
She struck her.
Inanna was turned into a corpse,
A piece of rotting meat,
And was hung from a hook on the wall.

The Annunaki hoist her up behind the throne and hang her. This should be well-practiced beforehand in order to be able to do it quickly; we did it with an EMT's body-board.

When, after three days and three nights,
Inanna had not returned,
Ninshubur set up a lament for her by the ruins.

Ninshubur runs about frantically. She goes from person to person in the audience, shakes them, gestures wildly, bangs on walls as if they are doors, generally mimes making a ruckus.

She beat the drum for her in the assembled places.
She circled the houses of the gods.
She tore at her eyes; she tore at her mouth;
She tore at her thighs.
She dressed herself in a single garment like a beggar.
Alone, she set out for Nippur and the temple of Enlil.

Ninshubur falls to her knees before Enlil's corner.

When she entered the holy shrine,
She cried out: "O Enlil, do not let your daughter
Be put to death in the underworld.
Yet it must be done.
Do not let your bright silver
Be covered with dust of the underworld.
Yet it must be done.
Do not let your precious lapis
Be broken into stone for the stoneworker.
Yet it must be done.
Do not let your fragrant boxwood
Be cut into wood for the woodworker.
Yet it must be done.

Do not let the holy priestess of heaven
Be put to death in the underworld."
Yet it must be done.

Enlil gestures imperiously and finally turns his back on her.

Enlil answered angrily: "My daughter had the Great Above.
But Inanna craved the Great Below.
She who receives the me of the underworld does not return.
She who goes to the Dark City stays there."
Enlil would not help.

Ninshubur runs to the other side of the area and flings herself on her knees in Nanna's corner.

Ninshubur went to Ur and the temple of Nanna.
When she entered the holy shrine,
She cried out:
"Oh Nanna, do not let your daughter
Be put to death in the underworld.
Yet it must be done.
Do not let your bright silver
Be covered with dust of the underworld.
Yet it must be done.
Do not let your precious lapis
Be broken into stone for the stoneworker.
Yet it must be done.
Do not let your fragrant boxwood
Be cut into wood for the woodworker.
Yet it must be done.
Do not let the holy priestess of heaven
Be put to death in the underworld."
Yet it must be done.

Nanna gestures imperiously at her and then finally turns his back on her.

Nanna answered angrily:
"My daughter had the Great Above.
But Inanna craved the Great Below.
She who receives the me of the underworld does not return.
She who goes to the Dark City stays there."
Nanna would not help.

Ninshubur runs to Enki's corner. Enki is just coming forward, reading a scroll, oblivious to her. Ninshubur throws herself at his feet and wraps her arms around his knees, pleading.

Ninshubur went to Eridu and the temple of Enki.
When she entered the holy shrine,
She cried out: "O Father Enki, do not let your daughter
Be put to death in the underworld.
Yet it must be done.
Do not let your bright silver
Be covered with dust of the underworld.
Yet it must be done.
Do not let your precious lapis
Be broken into stone for the stoneworker.
Yet it must be done.
Do not let your fragrant boxwood
Be cut into wood for the woodworker.
Yet it must be done.
Do not let the holy priestess of heaven
Be put to death in the underworld."
Yet it must be done.

Enki acts surprised, then gently disengages Ninshubur.

Father Enki said;
"What has happened?
What has my daughter done?
Inanna, Queen of All the Lands! Holy Priestess of Heaven!
What has happened? I am troubled, I am grieved."
For no man nor woman
Can enter the Underworld and live,
No man nor woman, and not even I, Enki,
The great god of Invention,
But I know who can!

Enki makes magical gestures, waving first one hand and then the other. From where they have been crouched under rough brown blankets, being part of the earth, the Kurgarra and Galatur arise. They wear only simple white tunics.

From under his fingernail Father Enki brought forth dirt.
He fashioned the dirt into a Kurgarra,
A creature neither male nor female.
From under the fingernail of his other hand
He brought forth dirt.
He fashioned the dirt into a Galatur,
A creature neither male nor female.

Enki hands the water of life to one and the food of life to the other. During these lines, he mimes instructing them, and meanwhile Ereshkigal can be seen pacing back and forth in front of her throne, moaning, holding her belly, weeping, beating on things, and generally acting anguished.

He gave the food of life to the Kurgarra.
He gave the water of life to the Galatur, saying:
"Go to the underworld,
Enter the doors like flies,
Ereshkigal, the Queen of the Underworld, is moaning
With the cries of a woman about to give birth.

No linen is spread on her body.

Her breasts are uncovered.

Her hair swirls about her head like leeks.

For no one knows how terrible it is to be Death.

All curse Death, and no one loves Her,

And no one shows her compassion.

She takes all the Dead into her womb,

And rebirths them again,

With no mate, no midwife, no aid,

No loving hands to see her through,

And all we do is curse Her yet again.

Weep for her.

The queen will be pleased. She will offer you a gift.

Ask her only for the corpse

That hangs from the hook on the wall.

One of you will sprinkle the food of life on it.

The other will sprinkle the water of life.

Inanna will arise."

And remember this mystery, ye who stand before us:

Remember it well:

That when you are trapped in the land of Death,

That the food of life and the water of life

Lie in the hands of those who lie

Between man and woman.

The Kurgarra and Galatur walk toward the Underworld gates. Their way is blocked by the seven Annunaki, holding their rods horizontally. As they approach, the Annunaki step out of the way one by one.

The Kurgarra and the Galatur heeded Enki's words.

They set out for the underworld.

Like flies, they slipped through the cracks of the gates.

They come into Ereshkigal's presence, where she has taken to her throne and is rocking back and forth, her arms wrapped around herself, miming weeping. She has torn half of her clothing off and is disheveled.

They entered the throne room
Of the Queen of the Underworld.
No linen was spread on her body.
Her breasts were uncovered.
Her hair swirled around her head like leeks.
Will no one ever have compassion for Death?
Shame on you all, who stand here now!
Can you not reach beyond your own small lives?

The Kurgarra and Galatur kneel before her throne. As she moans and rocks, they mime compassionate gestures and weep for her.

Ereshkigal was moaning: "Oh! Oh! My inside!"
They moaned. "Oh! Oh! Your inside!"
She moaned: "Oh! Oh! My outside!"
They moaned: "Oh! Oh! Your outside!"
She groaned: "Oh! Oh! My belly!"
They groaned: "Oh! Oh! Your belly!"
She groaned: "Oh! Oh! My back!"
They groaned: "Oh! Oh! Your back!"
She sighed: "Ah! Ah! My heart!"
They sighed: "Ah! Ah! Your heart!"
She sighed: "Ah! Ahhhh! My liver!"
They sighed: "Ah! Ahhhh! Your liver!"
And they wept for her, with the first tears that had ever been shed at her throne out of compassion and not fear. They wept, and for once Death was astonished.

Ereshkigal stops, rises, and walks over to them. She offers them a chalice of water; they refuse. She offers them a sheaf of grain; they refuse.

Ereshkigal stopped. She looked at them.

She asked: "Who are you,

Moaning—groaning—sighing with me?

If you are gods, I will bless you.

If you are mortals, I will give you a gift.

I will give you the water-gift, the river in its fullness."

The Kurgarra and Galatur answered: "We do not wish it."

For we carry the water of life in our hands,

The source of all waters.

Ereshkigal said: "I will give you the grain gift,

The fields in harvest."

The Kurgarra and Galatur said: "We do not wish it."

For we carry the food of life in our hands,

The source of all nourishment.

Ereshkigal said: "Speak then! What do you wish?"

They point to where Inanna hangs limply.

They answered: "We wish only for the corpse

That hangs from the hook on the wall."

Ereshkigal turns and walks over to where Inanna hangs. She appears to be studying the situation.

Ereshkigal said: "That corpse belongs to Inanna."

They said: "Whether it belongs to our queen,

Whether it belongs to our king,

That is what we wish."

Ereshkigal gestures and the Annunaki take Inanna down. She is motionless and limp, and they arrange her naked on the floor.

And so the Queen of Heaven
Was ransomed from Death
By the gift of tears,
Given to one who most think does not deserve them.
Remember this, ye who stand here before us,
Remember this when you are someday
Trapped in the Underworld.
Remember the gift of tears,
And ask who is undeserving?
The corpse was given to them.

The Kurgarra and Galatur sprinkle the food and water of life on Inanna. She slowly comes to life and rises, with accompanying fast drumbeats. They clothe her in a simple white robe, of the same fabric as their own simple white tunics.

The kurgarra sprinkled the food of life on the corpse.
The galatur sprinkled the water of life on the corpse.
Inanna rose...
But there is always a price.
No one walks away from Death for free.

The Annunaki seize Inanna's arms and do not let her follow the Kurgarra and Galatur.

Inanna was about to ascend from the underworld
When the Annunaki,
The judges of the underworld, seized her.
They said: "No one ascends from the underworld unmarked.
If Inanna wishes to return from the underworld,
She must provide someone in her place."

They let go of Inanna, but remain surrounding her. At this point, the participants shift from being the Annunaki to being the galla, the demons of the Underworld. They may don horrible masks at this point.

As Inanna ascended from the underworld,
The galla, the demons of the underworld, clung to her side.

*Inanna walks forth in triumphal procession, flanked by the Kurgarra and the
Galatur, and followed by the horde of demons.*

The galla were demons who know no food,
Who know no drink,
Who eat no offerings, who drink no libations,
Who accept no gifts.
They enjoy no lovemaking.
They have no sweet children to kiss.
For is it not so that this is what we find
When we enter the Underworld?
We carry these demons with us,
They cling to our sides, and we cannot defeat them
Except with sacrifice.
They tear the wife from the husband's arms,
They tear the child from the father's knees,
They steal the bride from her marriage home.
They come between us and everything we love.

The procession circles the room three times.

The demons clung to Inanna.
The small galla who accompanied Inanna
Were like reeds the size of low picket fences.
The large galla who accompanied Inanna
Were like reeds the size of large picket fences.
The one who walked in front of Inanna was not a minister,
Yet he carried a sceptre.
The one who walked behind her was not a warrior,
Yet he carried a mace.

Ninshubur comes forth as Inanna and her procession reach the center of the area again. She throws herself at Inanna's feet. The demons make as if to take her, but Inanna holds onto Ninshubur and protects her, standing proudly against the demons.

Ninshubur waited outside the palace gates.
When she saw Inanna
Surrounded by the galla
She threw herself in the dust at Inanna's feet.
The galla said: "Walk on, Inanna,
We shall take Ninshubur in your place."
Inanna cried:
"No! Ninshubur is my constant support.
She is my sukkal who gives me wise advice.
She is my warrior who fights by my side.
She did not forget my words.
She set up a lament for my by the ruins.
She beat the drum for me at the assembly places.
She circled the houses of the gods.
She tore at her eyes, at her mouth, at her thighs.
She dressed herself in a single garment like a beggar.
Alone she set out for Nippur and the temple of Enlil.
She went to Ur and the temple of Nanna.
She went to Eridu and the temple of Enki.
Because of her, my life was saved.
I will never give Ninshubur to you."

They walk on. Ninshubur runs ahead through the audience, crying out, "Welcome the Queen of Heaven! Welcome the Queen of Heaven!" She encourages people to bow to Inanna as she walks by. Dumuzi ascends Inanna's throne, which has been empty up until now. He places a crown on his head. When she approaches the throne, he acts surprised.

The galla said: "Walk on to your city, Inanna.
We will go with you to the big apple tree in Uruk."
In Uruk, by the big apple tree,
Dumuzi, the husband of Inanna,
Was dressed in his shining garments.
He sat on his magnificent throne.
And when he looked upon her,
She whom he had been told was dead,
Whom he had been told was lost to the Underworld,
Whose throne he had taken for himself
And was beginning to like that very much,
All he could think of to say was:
"You! What are you doing here?"

Inanna sees Dumuzi's reaction and becomes enraged.

Inanna fastened on Dumuzi the eye of death.
I come back from death,
And you do not greet me with joy and love?
She spoke against him the word of wrath.
I crawl back from torment in the Underworld,
And you do not care?
She uttered against him the cry of guilt.
"Take him away! Take Dumuzi away!"
My love, how could you do this to me!

*The demons rush over and seize Dumuzi. They drag him off the throne and
throw him down, and slap him around. The bind his wrists and pull his tunic up
over his head. They whip him, and torture his genitals.*

Inanna handed over Dumuzi to them
In exchange for herself.
For the wrath of a lover scorned will shake the world.
They cried, "We will put his feet in foot stocks!
We will put his hands in hand stocks,
We will put his neck in neck stocks!"
For his lack of compassion, he was bound.
The galla, who know no food, who know no drink,
Who eat no offerings, who drink no libations,
Who accept no gifts, seized Dumuzi.
They sharpened their large copper axes.
They gashed him with axes.
Copper pins, nails and pokers were raised to his face.
For his lack of love, he was the meat of demons.
They made him stand up, they made him sit down.
They bound his arms, they did evil to him.
They covered his face with his own garment.
They seized him by the thighs.
They beat the husband of Inanna.
They poured milk out of his seven churns.
They broke the reed pipe which the shepherd was playing.
For his numbness to the pain of others, he suffered.
Dumuzi let out a wail.
He raised his hands to heaven to Utu, the God of Justice,
And beseeched him:
"O Utu, you are my brother-in-law,
I am the husband of your sister.
I brought cream to your mother's house,
I brought milk to Ningal's house.
I am the one who carried food to the holy shrine.
I am the one who brought wedding gifts to Uruk
I am the one who danced on the holy knees,
The knees of Inanna.

Utu, you who are a just god, a merciful god,

Change my hands into the hands of a snake.

Change my feet into the feet of a snake.

Let me escape from my demons;

Do not let them hold me

Like a sajkal snake

That slithers across the meadows and mountains,

Let me escape alive

To the dwelling of my sister Geshtinanna!"

Geshtinanna will protect me.

More than anyone, she has always protected me.

She will suffer for me

So that I will not have to suffer for Inanna.

Dumuzi slips out of the bonds and away from the demons, and runs through the audience. The demons run after him, but cannot find him. Geshtinanna comes forward while the demons are busy in the audience, and they meet in the center and embrace.

The merciful Utu accepted Dumuzi's tears.

He changed the hands of Dumuzi into snake hands.

He changed the feet of Dumuzi into snake feet.

Dumuzi escaped from his demons.

Hunt him! Hunt him!

Then like a sajkal snake

That slithers across the meadows and mountains,

Hunt him! Hunt him!

Like a soaring falcon that can swoop down on a bird,

Hunt him! Hunt him!

Dumuzi escaped alive

To the dwelling of his sister Geshtinanna.

Geshtinanna looked at her brother and wept for him.

Oh my brother, what have you done?

Oh, my foolish brother,
You have all the demons of the Dead behind you.
Oh my foolish brother, I will save you anyway,
Even though you do not deserve it.

The demons mime searching for Dumuzi, then one steps forth and gestures,
and they clap their hands and go toward Geshtinanna. She motions for Dumuzi
to run away, and he hides in the audience.

The demons went hither and thither searching for Dumuzi.
The small demons said to the big demons:
"Who has ever seen a man, without a family,
All alone, escape with his life?
Let us go to the dwelling of Geshtinanna, his sister."
The demons clapped their hands and began to seek him out.
He will never escape us.
He will never escape us.
He will never escape us.
Geshtinanna had barely finished her lament
When the demons arrived at her dwelling.
"Show us where your brother is," they said to her.

The demons rush in and seize Geshtinanna, flinging her to the ground on her
hands and knees. They slap her around a bit.

He can never escape us.
But she spoke not a word to them.
They afflicted her loins with a disease,

The demons mime raping her.

He can never escape us.
But she spoke not a word to them.
They scratched her face with their nails,

The demons scratch at her and slap her around some more.

He can never escape us.
But she spoke not a word to them.
They whipped the skin of her buttocks,

The demons whip her.

He can never escape us.
But she spoke not a word to them.
They poured tar in her lap,

The demons pour candle wax over her.

He can never escape us.
But she spoke not a word to them.
So they could not find Dumuzi at the house of Geshtinanna.

The demons throw her down in disgust and walk away.

He can never escape us.
The small demons said to the big demons:
"Come, let's go to the holy sheepfold!"

The demons rush around through the audience, hunting. Dumuzi hides behind audience members.

He can never escape us.
There at the holy sheepfold they caught Dumuzi.

One of the demons points at him, and waves to the others.

He can never escape us.
They went hither and thither until they caught him.

The demons surround him with weapons held high.

He can never escape us.
They searched for him until he was seen.
He can never escape us.
The axe was wielded against the lad
Who had no longer any family.
He can never escape us.

The demons close in, slowly, about to smash him.

They sharpened their daggers, they smashed his hut.
His doom is upon him.
His doom is upon him.
His doom is upon him.

Geshtinanna runs toward the place where the demons have converged on Dumuzi.

His sister wandered about the city like a bird
Because of her brother:
"My brother, let me take the great misfortune,
Come, let me take this on for you!"

Geshtinanna flings herself in front of him.

Wait!
One offers her life for his!

The demons freeze, spears and axes lifted. Dumuzi falls to the ground. Inanna comes forward, and both she and Geshtinanna kneel beside him.

Inanna and Geshtinanna went to the edges of the steppe.

They found Dumuzi weeping.

Inanna took Dumuzi by the hand and said:

"You will go to the underworld half the year.

Your sister, since she has asked, will go the other half.

On the day you are called,

That day you will be taken.

On that day Geshtinanna is called,

That day you will be set free.

Half a life for half a life.

Half a life lived in the light,

Half a life lived in the darkness.

Inanna raises Dumuzi to his feet.

Inanna placed Dumuzi in the hands of the eternal.

Inanna leads him to the demons and hands him over. He obeys limply, as if exhausted.

And Death comes for him.

The demons leap upon him and he falls. They mime killing him with various blows. During the next lines, they slowly lift his body up and carry it off into the darkness as if to a funeral pyre. Geshtinanna drops to her knees and touches her forehead to the earth. Inanna stands, looking after him until he is gone, then turns and leads the procession out. All fall in behind her except for the narrators, who continue reading until the end. Everyone who walks out hums a note, like a wordless chant.

On the day when Dumuzi arises again,

And the lapis pipe and the carnelian ring come up with him,

When all the mourners weep for him,

The dead shall come up and smell the smoke offering.

For all of us, in our own time,

Must descend to the Underworld and arise.

Perhaps we go willing, perhaps unwilling,

But in the end it is the same place.

Hail the Queen of Heaven, for she has arisen from the dark!

Hail the Queen of Heaven!

And hail also those who take her place,

Hail all who descend to the darkness!

Hail all who descend to the darkness!

Hail all who descend to the darkness!

Hail all who descend to the darkness!

Silence descends, except for the booming of the drum.

Epilogue

For now, we have come to the end of our journey into the world of these two Goddesses. The next steps lie with you, the reader. The best way to honor Them is to honor Them: in word, in thought, in prayer, in deed. Set up an altar, pray to Them. Make regular offerings. Write your own prayers and invocations. Call upon Them in honor and celebration. Call upon Them in need. Give Them your time. Bring Them gifts and praise Them. Praise Their names, always. This is a holy restoration. It is a reclaiming of sacred things long ago lost. It is the tearing open of a door wrongly barred.

Below, I have listed a handful of books that might be useful in learning a little bit more about the Deities honored in this devotional. The list is far from complete, but it is a place to begin.

Finally, if I can but distill what these Goddesses have taught me, it is simple:

Honor Inanna by honoring life.

Honor Ereshkigal by honoring the Dead.

And in between: Praise Their names.

Bibliography

Frymer-Kensky, Tikvah, (1992). *In the Wake of the Goddesses*. NY: Fawcett Columbine.

Jacobsen, Thorkild, (1970). *The Treasures of Darkness*. New Haven, CT: Yale University Press.

Kaldera, Raven, (2006). *Dark Moon Rising*. Hubbardston, MA: Asphodel Press.

Muten, Burleigh, (editor), (1999). *Her Words*. Boston: Shambala.

Stone, Merlin, (1976). *When God Was a Woman*. San Diego, CA: Harcourt Brace & Company.

Wolkstein, Diane and Kramer, Samuel, (1983). *Inanna: Queen of Heaven and Earth*. NY: Harper & Row.

Sumerian Mythology: http://home.comcast.net/~chris.s/sumer-faq.html

And for the culinarily- inclined:

Kaufman, Cathy, (2006). *Cooking in Ancient Civilizations*. Westport, CT: Greenwood Press.

This book has an entire section on traditional Sumerian food culture and dishes as reconstructed from extant sources by food historians. Some would make excellent offerings.

About the Editor

Galina Krasskova is a Heathen priest, shaman, and *godatheow* of Odin, Loki and Sigyn. Originally ordained in the Fellowship of Isis, she currently runs Urdabrunnr Kindred in NY, and teaches for the College of Brigantia, part of the First Kingdom Church of Asphodel in Massachusetts. She holds a diploma in interfaith ministry from The New Seminary, a BA in cultural studies with a concentration in religious studies from Empire State College, and an MA in Religious Studies from New York University. She is the author of several books, including *Exploring the Northern Tradition*, *The Whisperings of Woden*, and *Day Star and Whirling Wheel*. She may be reached at Krasskova@gmail.com.